Jon Ronson
Out of the Ordinary:
True Tales of Everyday Craziness

PICADOR

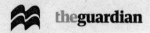

theguardian

First published 2006 by Picador
an imprint of Pan Macmillan Ltd
Pan Macmillan, 20 New Wharf Road, London N1 9RR
Basingstoke and Oxford
Associated companies throughout the world
www.panmacmillan.com

ISBN-13: 978-0-330-44832-1
ISBN-10: 0-330-44832-3

This book is published in association with Guardian Books.
Guardian Books is an imprint of Guardian Newspapers Limited.
The Guardian is a registered trademark of Guardian Media Group plc.

9 8 7 6 5 4 3 2 1

A CIP catalogue record for this book is available from
the British Library.

Typeset by Intype London Ltd
Printed and bound in Great Britain by
Mackays of Chatham plc, Chatham, Kent

Out of the Ordinary:
True Tales of Everyday Craziness

Jon Ronson is an award-winning writer
and documentary maker. He is the author
of two bestsellers: *Them: Adventures with
Extremists* and *The Men Who Stare at
Goats*. He lives in London.

Also by Jon Ronson

THEM: ADVENTURES WITH EXTREMISTS

THE MEN WHO STARE AT GOATS

To Elaine and Joel

CONTENTS

PREFACE AND ACKNOWLEDGEMENTS

This book begins in 2002 with me promising my four-year-old son Joel that I would stay with him in a Santa costume for the rest of his life. It was, on reflection, among my more stupid acts of parenting. Still, I contend that anyone might have made the same mistake had they taken their eye off the ball for a moment. A few hours later, as I explained to Joel that I was getting a rash, and he ought to prepare himself because I was about to take the beard off, I looked at myself as if from above and realized I'd become the kind of person I've been writing about all these years.

For years I've been writing about Klansmen and paranoid militant Islamists and extreme conspiracy theorists, people who believe that the world is run by giant lizards who've adopted human form, and US military intelligence chiefs who attempt to kill goats just by staring at them. These people had created for themselves bubbles within which all kinds of crazy thoughts and actions made perfect sense. One thought would spiral into another thought, and before long it was obvious to them that goats could be killed with a look.

It is easy for us more settled, secular, cosmopolitan type of people to look at the goat-starers and lizard-believers and see them as lunatics with character traits that are impossible to relate to. But I too was creating one of those crazy bubbles, only in a more ordinary, domestic setting. It had begun with me attempting to provide my son with an enchanting Christmas, and then one thing spiralled into another, and before I knew it I was making an insanely ill thought-out and possibly emotionally damaging promise about staying with him, in the guise of Santa, forever.

And so I started writing stories and columns about more ordinary craziness taking place in recognizable landscapes. This is a collection of these stories. They all first appeared, in different forms, in the *Guardian*'s *Weekend* magazine, although I've added postscripts here and there.

In Part One I've gathered together the stories I've written about my own moments of domestic craziness. In Part Two I've collected some stories I've written about other people – how one thing led to another, and before long extraordinary acts were occurring.

There are a few stories that don't immediately seem

to fit and consequently, I think, need some explanation as to why they've been included.

'The Fall of a Pop Impresario' tells of my year with the pop mogul Jonathan King as he faced trial for a series of child-sex offences. Unlike most of the other people in the book, one would be hard pressed to see Jonathan King and his friends as basically good-hearted people gone temporarily askew. (Another exception, in terms of likeability, is Dave McKay, the leader of the Jesus Christians. On a personal level, I like Dave less than anyone I've ever interviewed.) But I was interested in the bubble of self-delusion Jonathan King and his friends had created for themselves. The bubble is known, I suppose, as a show-business paedophile ring. Inside it they had convinced themselves that all manner of unpleasant, exploitative, selfish behaviour was perfectly OK. And that's exactly how they see their detractors – the police, the victims, the courts, unfriendly journalists – as a bubble filled with people who had irrationally convinced themselves that their innocent behaviour was unpleasant, exploitative and selfish.

I probably wouldn't have included the story 'Blood Sacrifice' had it not been for the extraordinary events that occurred as a result of the article appearing in the *Guardian*. I've detailed what happened in a long postscript.

The other story that might seem out of place is 'Citizen Kubrick'. This is about my months looking through the boxes Stanley Kubrick left behind at his home near St Albans. I see this as the book's happy ending: Kubrick did build for himself a world inside his house that may seem crazy by the standards of outsiders, but as a result he created some of the most wonderful films ever produced. So these bubbles can sometimes be far from malign or silly. They can be great.

Thanks to Kath Viner, Helen Oldfield, Melissa Denes, Hannah Pool, Bob Granleese, Billy Mann, Ritchie Parrott, Merope Mills, Lisa Darnell, Justine Picardie, Nick Hornby, William Fiennes, Sarah Harvey, Stephen Gill, Ira Glass, Jonathan Bernstein, Alex Blumberg, John Hodgman, Geoff Kloske, Sarah Vowell, Ursula Doyle, Camilla Elworthy, Derek Johns, Christine Glover, and Nick Harris.

This book would be dedicated to Katie, Ed, Kellie, Shirley, Sam and the others from jonronson.com had I not dedicated it to Elaine and Joel.

PART ONE

1. A FANTASTIC LIFE

It is a Friday in December. I have now been dressed as Santa for five hours. The heating in our house is on full blast. The costume was itchy when I put it on all those hours ago. Now I feel as if I am covered in ants. 'I need to take the beard off,' I say.

'No!' says Joel, my four-year-old son.

'I'm getting a rash,' I say.

'Please stay with me, Santa,' says Joel.

The original plan had been to creep up behind Joel dressed as Santa. I'd say, 'Ho! Ho! Ho!' We would laugh about it, then I'd take off the costume and we'd go back to normal. But it didn't work out that way. Although Joel knew it was me, he was so thrilled to have his own personal Santa that he didn't want it to end. Three hours ago, he whispered, 'Will you stay with me for ever, Santa?'

I replied, 'Yes, I will. For ever and ever and ever.'

*

'I think I may be allergic to whatever fabric they make the beard out of,' I say now.

'Don't go, Santa,' says Joel. 'Don't leave me.'

I give my wife, Elaine, an imploring look. She shrugs and goes downstairs to the kitchen. She thinks I have nobody to blame for this but myself.

'I think I'm getting hives,' I say. 'I'm feeling very claustrophobic.'

'No, Santa, no!' says Joel.

'I need air,' I gasp. 'I need air.'

I am having a panic attack dressed as Santa.

'Prepare yourself, because I am going to take the beard off . . . now!' I say.

I do. Joel runs from the room. I go upstairs to my office for a cigarette.

In my office I log on to Friends Reunited. A few weeks ago I decided to track down the boys who threw me into Roath Park Lake in Cardiff in the summer of 1983 when I was sixteen. In the middle of the night a few Saturdays ago I woke up and realized I was still angry about what they did. I found one of them and emailed to inform him that I am now a bestselling author.

He emailed me back within a few hours. He told me that the reason why they threw me in the lake back then was that I was a pain in the arse. He added that the tenor of my email leads him to suspect that I haven't changed, and that throwing me in the lake again today would be an appropriate response. I emailed him back to say that I earn more money than he does. He has not yet emailed me back.

Touché.

'Santa,' Joel yells from downstairs.

'Coming!' I shout.

My plan is to give Joel the most perfect Christmas imaginable. This is part of my overall strategy to provide him with a constantly enchanting childhood. I don't want to blow my own trumpet, but I think I provide magical moments for Joel in a far more unremitting way than my parents did for me. I rarely stop, and then only to go upstairs for cigarettes.

Nonetheless, at times like this, when every synthetic fibre of this cheap Santa suit feels as though it's snaking its way inside my skin, and I realize that I've been adopting a Santa tone of voice throughout my argument with Joel – even when I told him I might be allergic to the beard fabric, I said it with a 'Ho! Ho! Ho!' type of booming twinkle – I see myself lucidly, from above, and I recognize that I wasn't like this when he was a baby. I was averagely delightful in those days, entrancing in a manner that would not seem unusual when written down.

*

Outside the school gates, all the parents speak of their plans to give their children the most perfect Christmas imaginable. Perhaps I'll bump into some of them in Lapland next week. One mother looks tense. She tells me that her four-year-old son asked her last night if he's going to die.

'What did you say?' I ask.

'I said, "You won't ever die,"' she says. 'And then he said, "What about you and Daddy? Will either of you ever die?" And I said, "No. We will never die, either. None of us will ever die."'

She looks at me. I shrug. We are like amateur bomb-disposal officers, forever cutting the wrong wires.

I take Joel to a Christmas party. Another father is fighting over something with his four-year-old son. The boy screams, stands up, pushes his father out of the door and slams it. The father is left in the corridor. He chooses to stay there. Nobody goes to check if he's OK. Is he sitting out there with his head in his hands?

The Lapland trip is a few days away. The brochure says we will take a husky ride, a reindeer ride, a snowmobile ride and a toboggan ride and meet Santa in a snowy cabin in the middle of a pine forest. I'm not paying for the trip. I am writing it up as a travel article for the *Guardian*. This means I'll be able to provide Joel with a magical and unforgettable Christmas, do it for free and give him a gift that money can't buy – the gift of fame. The *Guardian* is sending a photographer, Barry Lewis, to Lapland to take pictures of Joel with Santa, and he will be the cover star of the paper's *Weekend* magazine's Christmas edition. We'll keep it, and in years to come he'll be impressed that his father was in a position to get him on the front cover of a magazine.

As a precursor, I decide to take Joel to Santa's Kingdom at Wembley. The advert makes it look wonderful – a drawing of a shimmering, snowy, chocolate-box village somehow recreated inside Wembley Exhibition Halls 1 and 2. The official website includes a visitor's diary written by a seven-year-old called Mary T. Moore. She writes: 'December 12 2002. We all checked in and were given our wristbands, which were bright blue in colour! Elf street was kool. Santa was exactly like he is in all the photos and he does eat too much chocolate. We played in the snowball alley and mum went shopping.'

Although her diary was written about her December 12 visit, it was posted on santaskingdom.co.uk on November 29. This is unnerving. Could Mary T. Moore not exist? Such marketing deceits are acceptable in the realms of everyday adult pursuits, but I am trying to construct a perfect Christmas for my four-year-old and I am in no mood to be fucked with. In the absence of an actual foe to protect my son against, I am forever attuned to the possibility of outsiders carelessly puncturing the ambience of constant enchantment that I have created around him.

I decide to not tell Joel that we're going to Santa's Kingdom. I opt to make it a magical mystery tour instead. In the taxi on the way to Wembley, Joel interrogates me for clues to our destination.

'It is Body Worlds, isn't it?' he says. 'Hooray! We're finally going to Body Worlds!'

Body Worlds is a travelling exhibition of pickled human remains.

'It isn't Body Worlds,' I say.

Joel's face crumbles.

'I want to go to Body Worlds,' he cries.

'Listen,' I say, crossly, 'if you're naughty we're going straight into town to see *Stomp* again.'

'No!' yells Joel, genuinely alarmed. 'Not *Stomp* again. Please not *Stomp* again.'

This threat works for a few minutes. Then Joel starts again. 'If we don't go to Body Worlds,' he explains, 'I'm going to keep saying shit.'

'Joel,' I warn, 'we are not going to Body Worlds.'

'You're worse than Jonathan King,' he yells.

The taxi driver peers at us in his rear-view mirror. I wish I'd never told Joel that Jonathan King – whose music Joel admires – is in prison for being naughty to boys.

'Shit!' says Joel.

I resort to the ace in my pack, the one thing that invariably makes Joel behave well. '*Jesus* wouldn't have said shit,' I say, 'and *Jesus* wouldn't have wanted to go to Body Worlds.'

Joel loves Jesus. I don't know where this came from, but I suspect it might be from a trailer for a cartoon called *The Lamb of God* on the video of *Scooby Doo and the Witch's Ghost*. We are not a religious family. Like many people, I've relinquished pretty much every aspect of Western living that could be described as 'being part of something bigger than myself'. I am not a member of a union. I don't go to synagogue. The only clubs I'm a member of are the gym, where I don't talk to anyone, and the Randy Newman online fan club, which I rarely log on to. When I was a child, my father, like most people of his generation, spread his well of enchanting-ness around the various clubs to which he belonged. He was a little enchanting at the golf club, a little enchanting at the bridge club and a little enchanting at home. But I concentrate the entirety of my enchanting-ness on Joel.

Santa's Kingdom turns out to be an extremely regimented snowy paradise. It is packed. We are shepherded by strict elves from one tiny room to another, where costumed actors sing us songs or tell us jokes before we are ushered on. Every few minutes a magic-skewering announcement comes over the PA: 'Will the solid aqua wristbands please leave Santa's Kingdom *now*.'

'I'm getting rather old,' says the toymaker to the crowd. 'I'm beginning to think of Ann Widdecombe as a sexy young thing!'

There are blank faces from children and adults alike.

Joel's mind wanders, and he starts playing with the props. An elf appears at his side within half a second. 'Stay away from the toy machine,' says the elf. Joel obeys at once. He seems comforted by this unambiguous order. There are, in fairness, a few good bits about Santa's Kingdom: a wishing well that talks to you – not a recorded voice but a real conversation – and a snow slide we're allowed to go down exactly three times. Three little boxes on our wristbands are ticked off after each go. But the whole thing is claustrophobic, and the rigid structure squeezes all fun out of it. Had it been one vast kingdom where we could roam freely, as opposed to a warren of little rooms with no grand climax, it might have been better.

'What Christmas present would you like this year?' the toymaker asks Joel on our way out.

'Um . . .' says Joel, frantically. 'Um—'

'Oh good, lots and lots,' interrupts the toymaker. He turns to someone else.

'A rescue castle,' yelps Joel. But it is too late. We no longer have the toymaker's attention.

There is a silence.

'Do you think he heard me?' asks Joel.

'Were you once thrown in a lake?' Joel asks later, back at home.

'Yes,' I say. 'I was thrown in a lake in Cardiff when I was sixteen.'

'Why?' he asks.

'Because I was fat,' I explain. 'I was fat when I was sixteen. And that's why they threw me in the lake.'

'Wow!' he says.

'There are two lessons to be learnt from this,' I say. 'Don't be a bully and don't be fat.'

He thinks about this.

'Will you show me what it looked like?' he asks.

'Me being fat or me being thrown in a lake?' I ask.

'Both,' he says.

I puff up my cheeks, waddle comically around the room for a moment, fall over and say, 'Splash!'

There is a silence.

'Will you do it again in slow motion?' asks Joel.

So I do. This time I add some dialogue: 'Please don't throw me in the lake! Nooooooo! Splash.'

'Will you sound more scared,' says Joel, 'and put a cushion under your shirt.'

So I do.

'*Please!*' I shout, waddling grotesquely. 'I might drown. Please! No, No. *No! No!*'

There is a silence.

'You were *so* fat!' says Joel.

Joel asks me to do it one final time. He is like Sam Peckinpah, forever directing me to make it more grotesque. He wants me to mime the swallowing of dirty water as I struggle to the surface. I go too far when I simulate a death rattle. This visibly upsets him. He wants to see me retain some dignity.

Northern Finnish Lapland. Sunday night. There are five of us. This is a mini-Arctic expedition. There is Sammy, our local guide and driver. There's Barry, the *Guardian*'s photographer. There's Elaine. There's Joel. And there's me. It is 7.30 p.m. Sammy has just picked us up from Kuusamo Airport. We have not yet reached our log cabin in nearby Ruka – our home for the next three nights. Instead, Sammy has driven us to an equipment-hire shop, a hut in a forest, where we are fitted with snowsuits. We run around outside for a few minutes, throwing snow at each other. Joel has never touched real snow before. He is amazed. But the seven-hour journey (two planes and a two-hour connection at Helsinki airport) has tired him out.

'Can I go to bed now?' he asks the adults.

Sammy smiles enigmatically. 'Maybe,' he says, 'there is something more exciting than sleep tonight. Maybe there will be an amazing Christmas adventure.'

'First I'm going to have an amazing sleeping adventure,' says Joel, cheerfully. 'Then I'll have an amazing Christmas adventure tomorrow.'

'Maybe not,' laughs Sammy. 'Maybe the adventure will begin tonight.'

I take Sammy to one side. 'What's going on?' I ask.

'Joel must meet Santa tonight!' he whispers, urgently. 'There's a horse-drawn sleigh parked outside your cabin right now, and it's going to take you through the forest to another cabin, and Santa is already there, hidden, waiting for Joel.'

Joel yawns, happily unaware of the unfolding crisis. Elaine has overheard some of this conversation, and she gives me a panicked stare that says, 'For Christ's sake, get them to postpone Santa.'

'Joel's very tired,' I say. 'Can we not meet Santa in the morning? We're jet-lagged and we need to unpack and acclimatize.'

'That is impossible,' says Sammy, with a startling finality.

There is a silence.

'Perhaps the sight of the horse-drawn sleigh will perk Joel up,' I say.

The five of us climb into the minibus and drive through the snowy forest. We turn a corner, and all at once we gasp. Our cabin is covered in a blanket of thick snow. The surrounding pine trees glisten with snow, too, and a path of glowing candles lights up the driveway. A horse-drawn sleigh, complete with jingle bells and reindeer pelts, waits for us at the front door, as does the sleigh's driver. It is just about the loveliest thing I have ever seen.

'Bedtime!' yells Joel. He jumps out of the van, ignoring the one-horse open sleigh, and rushes, focused, into the warm cabin. I follow him inside. He has already found a double bed and has jumped into it, pulling the duvet up to his chin.

'This is a perfect bed,' he says. 'Good night.'

'I think,' I say, 'that somebody very special wants to meet you before you go to sleep.'

Joel thinks about this for a moment.

'No,' he says.

I hurry outside. 'Sammy,' I say, 'we have a serious problem. Joel is already almost asleep. He's only four.'

'We do have a serious problem,' says Sammy, 'because Santa is only available immediately.'

Barry intercedes. 'Do you really want a picture of a scared, tired and crying child meeting Santa?' he asks.

'No,' says Sammy, 'but the schedule is inflexible.'

I notice, in the darkness behind the cabin, figures moving around. I don't know who they are. I assume they are shadowy cogs in this apparently complicated operation. I rush over to Elaine. 'They're not backing down!' I hiss.

'Oh God,' says Elaine.

'I'm not coming out,' yells Joel from the window.

I rush back inside.

'The horse is crying,' I tell Joel, 'because he's dying to meet you. He's crying now!'

'OK,' he says, 'I'll meet the horse. But that's it. Then I'm going straight back to bed.'

Together, Joel and I walk out into the snow.

'Hello,' says Joel, magnanimously, to the horse.

'Joel,' says Sammy, 'would you like to sit in the sleigh for a moment while you talk to the horse?'

Joel shoots Sammy a suspicious glance. Nonetheless, he climbs into the sleigh. I quickly jump in and throw a reindeer pelt over the two of us. Elaine and Barry pile hurriedly in behind us. 'Go!' I hiss. 'Go!'

The driver cracks the whip, and the horse trots lazily off down the snowy lane towards Santa. We fall into a wonderful silence. The jingle bells ring out magically with every step the horse takes. A stirring of Northern Lights pulsates above us as we ride through the shimmering pine trees. Joel's mood is lifted. He begins to sing 'Jingle Bells' to himself.

'It's just so beautiful,' I sigh. 'Isn't it, Joel? Isn't it perfect?'

Joel doesn't answer.

Behind me, Elaine and Barry begin to bitch incessantly. 'Would it have been too much to have asked for a negotiable timetable?' mutters Barry.

'It's just a nightmare,' agrees Elaine.

Barry and Elaine are working themselves up into something of a frenzy, out here amid the pine trees.

'People bring terminally ill children here,' says Elaine. 'You don't *force* a terminally ill child to meet Santa.'

'That's completely right,' says Barry.

We park up outside a log cabin and walk inside to discover that a vast banquet has been laid on for us. Joel takes one look at the meats and cookies and juice and salmon platter and he bursts into tears.

'You tricked me,' he wails, throwing himself underneath a pine bench and adopting a foetal position.

During crisis situations such as this, I usually attempt to alter Joel's mood by transforming myself into some kind of physical comedian, pulling out all the stops to provide instant enchantment. I use any prop to hand, interspersing my slapstick buffoonery with the yelling-out of positive statements such as 'You're extremely talented, Joel! You're going to be a great success in later life!' Instead, I whisper to Sammy, 'If Santa comes *right now* we may be OK.'

Sammy and I hurry outside to find a lovely old Santa, his eyes twinkling, rubbing his hands to keep warm inside a four-wheel-drive parked behind a tree.

'Hello!' he hollers.

'Let's do it now, Santa,' I say.

'OK,' says Santa.

I rush back to the cabin and dramatically fling open the door. Joel, noticing an escape opportunity, squeezes out from underneath the bench and makes a run for it, just as Santa appears from the darkness. Joel skids to a startled halt.

'Ho! Ho! Ho!' says Santa.

'Get them to stand next to each other,' urges Barry the photographer. 'I can't get them in the same frame.'

Santa takes a step towards Joel. Joel takes an anxious step backwards.

'He's demented with exhaustion,' whispers Elaine through gritted teeth.

'You're the best, Santa!' I shout as loudly as I can, trying to drown out all the negativity.

'They look like they're in different rooms,' mutters Barry, panicked.

'Joel! Do you think there's a mouse living in Santa's beard? Would you like to go and look?'

'This is making me very sad,' says Elaine.

'Oh, Santa, I'm so tired,' says Joel, giving him an imploring look, as if to say, 'If anyone can stop this madness, surely you can.'

'We all love you, Santa,' I screech.

Randy Newman was once asked about a song of his, 'I Love To See You Smile', the title theme to the movie *Parenthood*. 'It's the most lucrative song I ever wrote,' he said. 'I was able to hire a nanny to play with my children for me. So a movie about being a good parent allowed me to put even more distance between my children and myself.'

I think about this as I attempt to coerce the exhausted and hugely reluctant Joel towards Santa so Barry can get a decent photograph to accompany my article on perfect parenthood, which will earn me enough money to pay for Joel's nanny for another eight weeks. Then I shrug and think, Things have gone too far to stop now, and I ask Joel if he can spot the mouse in Santa's beard.

'Peace and quiet at last,' says Joel, back in his bed in the log cabin.

'Wasn't Santa lovely,' I say, trying to gauge the level of emotional scarring Joel has suffered in the past hour. Actually, he was a great Santa, a perfect Santa, unfazed by the chaos. Things did settle down after a while, with Joel telling Santa that his bedroom is the one with the two *Harry Potter* posters so he'll know where to leave the presents. But now, in bed, Joel's mind is on other things. He's thinking about a boy who is apparently something of a class bully. Two days before we set off for Lapland, by Joel's account, this boy shouted at him. In bed, Joel suddenly sits up and says, 'I'm going to have a horrible life.'

I gasp. 'No, you're not,' I say. 'You're going to have a fantastic life. Do you know why?'

'Why?' Joel asks.

'Because you're clever and funny,' I say. 'Clever, funny people have fantastic lives.'

Joel allows himself a small, optimistic smile. Elaine listens, unnoticed by me, from the doorway.

'In fact,' I add, thrilled that I'm doing so well, 'do you

know which people have horrible lives after leaving school? Bullies! Bullies leave school and have horrible lives, while special people like you have blessed, magical lives, where nothing bad happens at all.'

'Really?' asks Joel.

'Yes,' I say. 'Only bad things happen to bullies, and only good things happen to people like you.'

'Those were the worst bloody words of wisdom I've heard in my life,' shouts Elaine, furiously, later.

'What?' I say.

'First,' says Elaine, 'Joel won't automatically have a fantastic life. In fact, he'll probably have a worse life now because of the unrealistic expectations you've just instilled in him.'

'Oh God,' I say, horrified. 'He'll forget I said it, won't he?'

'And bullies don't automatically have terrible lives,' adds Elaine. 'What you just told Joel was warped and disturbing. You're teaching the boy Schadenfreude!'

Before Joel was born, I had a mental picture of what fatherhood might be like: my son and I were in a car together, driving down a motorway. We turned to each other and smiled. That was it. I notice now that this mental picture lacked dialogue.

Joel is out of bed, now too excited to sleep. Elaine, Barry and I drink cognac in front of the fire while Joel bounces around in front of us. 'Shit!' he sings, screeching across the room. 'Shit! Shit! Shit!'

'Peter, Susan, Edmund and Lucy didn't say shit in Narnia,' I say.

'You're good at the humour,' says Barry, who has raised four children, 'but a weakness in your parenting is control. Control is the weak spot.'

'Do you really think I'm good at the humour?' I ask, flattered.

'Yes,' says Barry.

'You said that in such a way as to imply that being good at the humour isn't enough,' I say.

Barry looks at me to see if I'm joking. When he realizes I'm not, he gives me a brief, pitying stare, and says nothing about my parenting skills again.

The next morning, Barry is worried. He never got a perfect shot of Joel and Santa together. He asks Sammy if the organization can broker another meeting, this time with more advance warning.

Sammy is concerned. 'But any Santa we manage to get now won't be the real Santa,' he says.

'Uh . . .' I say.

'Yes, yes,' says Sammy, cutting my obvious next question short. He reluctantly agrees to find a Santa to meet us at the reindeer farm tomorrow.

The next twenty-four hours are blissful. Sammy takes us husky-sleighing. We drink reindeer soup in a tepee in a frozen forest. We end the day with a snowmobile expedition across a frozen lake. The next morning, Sammy drives us to a reindeer farm. The reindeer takes Joel and me on a hair-raising sleigh ride across a field, kicking snow in Joel's face.

'That's it,' yells Joel, giving the reindeer and me a ferocious stare as if to say, 'I know the two of you plotted this together.'

I wipe the snow from Joel's face.

'I'm going to have a horrible life,' says Joel.

The reindeer-farmer's son, who can speak little English, disappears at lunchtime. He reappears a few moments later dressed as Santa. 'Look, Joel!' says Barry, raising his camera. 'Wow! How about that?'

'Hello again, Santa,' laughs Joel, excitedly. 'I didn't know you were coming to see me again.'

Santa nods, grumpily.

'I wonder if Santa has got a mouse living in his beard,' says Barry.

'It's lovely to see you,' says Joel.

Santa silently folds his arms, diffidently tapping his fingers against his coat.

'Santa,' says Joel, concerned, 'are you OK?'

'Santa has reindeer problems,' I say. 'Isn't that true, Santa? You've come to check on your reindeers because they're sick, that's why you're preoccupied.'

Santa grunts. Barry gets a lovely photograph of Joel posing with Santa.

Twenty-four hours later, and we're back in London. Joel's nanny, Francielly, is feeding the cat. She's there when we arrive home. Joel runs through the front door.

'Our log cabin,' he shrieks, 'had two toilets.'

'Really?' says Francielly.

'Two toilets!' sighs Joel, contentedly.

2. THE FAMILY PORTRAIT

My family runs a hotel – the Nant Ddu Lodge – in the Brecon Beacons mountain range of mid-Wales. I go home to the hotel every Christmas, and at some point I always manage to say, 'I treat this place just like a hotel!' and it always gets a big laugh.

Sometimes, famous people stay at the hotel. My mother always telephones me when it happens. When the TV news journalist John Cole was there recently, my mother phoned me up and said, 'Guess what? John Cole is staying here, and he hasn't heard of you.'

A few years ago, John Birt – then the Director General of the BBC – came in for lunch. My father approached his table: 'Are you John Birt?' he asked.

'Yes,' said John Birt.

'I wonder if you can help,' said my father. 'The TV reception in this area can be all crackly and fuzzy. Can you do anything about this?' I think my father wanted John Birt to get onto the roof and fix the aerial.

'We spoke about all sorts,' my father told me on the phone afterwards. 'The problems I'm having with my car – he couldn't believe that it's been in the garage six times.'

'Oh, and he hasn't heard of you,' added my mother, on the extension line.

Recently, my family won the coveted Welsh Hotel of the Year competition. It was a big honour, and they wanted to do something to commemorate the success. So they decided to commission a portrait-painter to immortalize the Ronsons.

'We've decided to have a group family portrait commissioned,' said my mother on the phone. 'A Ronson family portrait to be hung in the bar. Will you be available for a sitting?'

'Certainly,' I said. 'Who's doing it?'

'He's a brilliant but troubled local artist,' she said. 'He did the mural for the new Cardiff multiplex. You must have heard of it.'

'No,' I said.

'Oh, come on,' she said. 'It's been in all the papers.'

It turned out that the artist's particular sub-speciality is painting celebrities in classical Renaissance settings – such as Clint Eastwood ascending to heaven surrounded by angels. His ambition is to create the longest painting in the world, nearly a mile long, to be hung alongside the

M4 between London and Cardiff. It will depict celebrities such as Julia Roberts, Clint Eastwood and Tom Cruise in a kind of biblical tableau, like Raphael's *Martyrdom of St Matthew*. His loving recreations of celebrities set my parents thinking. So many famous people stay at their hotel. What if the Ronson family portrait was extended to include celebrities?

'Listen to this!' said my mother on the phone the next day. 'We, the family, will be standing in the grounds of the hotel, surrounded by famous people.'

'Which famous people?' I asked. 'You mean, the famous people who've stayed in the hotel?'

'Oh no,' said my mother. 'Any famous people. You have to choose your three famous people by Wednesday. We're working on a tight deadline. Send a Polaroid of yourself to the artist. And come up with three famous people. Living or dead. Comedians, statesmen, actors, anything.'

'Let me clarify this in my head,' I said.

'There's nothing to clarify,' said my mother.

'Don't you think it may come across as a little self-aggrandizing?' I asked.

'I'm choosing President Kennedy, Gandhi and Churchill,' said my mother.

My father came on to the phone.

'Who are you choosing?' I asked him.

'Gary Player, Arnold Palmer and Jack Nicklaus,' he said.

'All golfers?' I asked.

'So who are you choosing?' asked my father.

My mind drew a blank. In fact, I began to panic. I imagined, in hundreds of years' time, notable art historians gathered around the painting making sarcastic comments. Paintings are so permanent. I was to be frozen for eternity with three celebrities, and now the only question was: which celebrities best represented my essence? It was easy for my father. It was as if each of his three golfers portrayed a different subtlety to his personality. There was Arnold Palmer, the kind and thoughtful golfer with a common touch. There was Jack Nicklaus, the fiery, steely golfer who once said, 'Nobody ever remembers who finished second at anything.' And there was Gary Player, the philosophical golfer, whose ten commandments for life – as seen on garyplayer.com – include 'The fox fears not the man who boasts by night but the man who rises early in the morning.'

But who could I choose? I found myself feeling hostile to the whole idea, a hostility that manifested itself in a lazy choice of celebrities.

'I'm going for the Beverley Sisters,' I told my mother on the phone. I actually have no interest in girl groups of the 1950s, but I did know that the Beverley Sisters all looked exactly alike, and my choice was designed to be viewed by art historians of the future as an ironic silent protest.

'You can't have the Beverley Sisters,' said my mother, knowing me well enough to understand all this in an instant.

'How about Sister Sledge?' I said.

'Are you trying to ruin this?' said my mother.

I relented and opted for my real all-time celebrity hero: 'Randy Newman,' I said.

'Nobody knows what Randy Newman looks like,' she snapped.

In the end, we compromised – for all time, it would be Jon Ronson, Ike and Tina Turner, and Boris Yeltsin.

The Ronsons were going to be hobnobbing with the stars. The laws of physics tell us that one needs to be very careful approaching a star. If your trajectory and speed are just right, you'll go into orbit, safe and sound, glowing in the warm, beautiful starlight. If you mess up in any way – the wrong direction, the wrong speed – you'll hurtle into the face of the star and be vaporized; only the star will remain. My parents were involving us in a dangerous game.

A few days later, my mother called to tell me that the concept had changed slightly. Each Ronson, she said, would no longer just be standing and chatting to the celebrities. We were to be serving them drinks. This was, after all, a hotel. So now I was to be frozen in time in an act of subservience. To Boris Yeltsin. A few days later, the concept changed yet again. It was back to standing and chatting. But, this time, the Ronsons would be talking, and the celebrities would be listening.

'So you'll be talking,' I clarified, 'and Kennedy, Gandhi and Churchill will be listening?'

'What's the problem?' said my mother.

'Nothing,' I said. 'I'm just worried that people may get the wrong idea. You know, that we consider ourselves as good as Kennedy and . . .'

'What are you saying?' said my mother.

'Nothing,' I said.

I changed the subject. 'What will you be talking to Kennedy, Gandhi and Churchill about?'

'What do you mean, what will I be talking to them about?' said my mother. 'Nothing. I'm talking to them about nothing. It's a painting.'

'Maybe Dad will be talking to the golfers about the amount of times his car has been in the garage,' I suggested.

I sent in my Polaroids, and we all waited. Months passed. My father would telephone the artist from time to time to find out how things were going and when he was likely to be finished. Most often, the artist didn't even pick up the phone, and when he did he was a man of few words, which were spoken gruffly.

'Nearly there,' he said.

'Are you pleased with it so far?' asked my father.

'Don't worry,' said the artist.

My father began to worry.

The day of the grand unveiling came without warning. The artist just turned up one morning carrying a large canvas covered in a white sheet. He propped it up against the bar. The family gathered around it with a sense of great expectation. Everyone looked at the covered painting and at the artist, trying to read his facial expression. The artist said, 'I think you ought to know that I'm going through a creative stage that some people find difficult to connect to.'

There was a silence.

'What I'm saying,' he continued, 'is there's a possibility you may not like it.'

The Ronsons looked at one another. Then, with a flourish, the artist whipped off the sheet.

'There you go,' he said.

For a moment, the Ronsons just stared. My mother whispered, 'Oh my God.' She stormed out of the room. My brother and his wife followed, as a show of unity, slamming the door behind them.

The artist was left alone with my father. They didn't make eye contact. They just stared at the painting.

The famous people had all been painted with tender accuracy. There were a few celebrities – Clint Eastwood, Rowan Atkinson and Jennifer Saunders – whom none of the Ronsons had actually asked for, and many of the celebrities the Ronsons had requested were missing.

But that wasn't the problem. The problem was that, although the celebrities were lovingly depicted, the Ronsons stood among them as human grotesqueries, repulsive caricatures of monsters. My brother looked like Frankenstein's monster. He had a bolt through his neck. It was disturbing and humiliating. My parents looked like hastily sketched recovering drug addicts. I looked like a gawky, spotty adolescent, frozen in a gormless pose. But, unlike the other Ronsons, at least it did look a bit like me.

The painter had spent all those months making the celebrities look beatific, and he'd just whipped off the Ronsons really fast, as though he'd done them the night before, as a hostile afterthought. Plus, the Ronsons were utterly dwarfed by the celebrities – my brother was a small Frankenstein's monster, peeking out from behind Walter Matthau's hat.

'Sorry,' said the painter, looking at the floor.

'We're not paying for it,' said my father.

There was a long silence.

'It's just not, um, realistic enough,' said my father, attempting something conciliatory, as if the original idea of serving mint juleps to John F. Kennedy and Robert Mitchum was more realistic.

My father ordered the artist to paint the Ronsons out and, after much negotiation, he agreed. He turned my mother into Woody Allen. My father is now Jimmy Carter. I like to think the artist chose Jimmy Carter, the famed peacemaker, to replace my dad as a homage to my father's diplomacy – because he was the only Ronson who didn't storm out. My brother was turned into David Rockefeller and his wife was turned into Henry Kissinger, which I interpret as an act of hostility. The only Ronsons left in the portrait are, oddly, my wife, Elaine, and I. The painting now hangs between the cigarette machine and the coat stand of the bar in my family's hotel, and it is the cause of interest among the customers. They crowd around it, trying to guess who everyone is.

'That's Kennedy!' they say. 'Look, Jennifer Saunders.' Nobody gets David Rockefeller. I have to say, 'It's David Rockefeller.'

'Ah,' they reply, 'David Rockefeller.'

They stare blankly at the likeness of me, too, for

whole minutes at a time, trying to figure out who exactly I am.

'I've been on TV,' I say. But they all just squint and shrug.

If my mother's there, she'll say, 'Oh, they've never heard of you.'

3. MESSAGES FROM GOD

It's a Wednesday evening in early summer, and you'd think some high-society soirée was taking place in Knightsbridge, West London, on beautiful lawns set back from the Brompton Road. Porsches and Aston Martins are parked up, and attractive young people, some with famous names, in casual wear and summer dresses are wandering up a tree-lined drive. But this is no soirée.

We are agnostics. We are entering a church – the Holy Trinity Brompton (HTB) – to sign up for the Alpha Course, led by Nicky Gumbel. He is over there, welcoming agnostics; he's good-looking, tall and slim. It sounds impossible, but apparently Gumbel's course, consisting of ten Wednesday evenings, routinely transforms hardened unbelievers, the entrenched faithless, into confirmed Christians. There will be after-dinner talks from Gumbel, and then we will split into small groups to discuss the meaning of life, etc. There will be a weekend away in Kidderminster. And that's it. Salvation will occur within these parameters. I cannot imagine how it can work.

However, at a cautious estimate, in Britain alone and in less than a decade, a quarter of a million agnostics have found God through Nicky Gumbel. To name one: Jonathan Aitken. 'I am a man of unclean lips,' he told the Catholic newspaper the *Tablet*, 'but I went on an Alpha Course at Holy Trinity Brompton, and found great inspiration from its fellowship and the teachings on the Holy Spirit.' The *Tablet* added, 'He has done Alpha not once but three times, graduating from a humble student to a helper who pours coffee.'

Nicky Gumbel's supporters say that within Church of England circles he is now more influential than the Archbishop of Canterbury; they claim that Alpha is saving the Church. Other people say some quite horrifying things about him. I was told it is almost impossible to get an interview with him. His diary was full for three years. His people were apologetic. They said that the only way to really get to know Nicky, to understand how he does it, was to enrol in Alpha.

'Hi!' says a woman wearing a name tag. 'You're . . .?'

'Jon Ronson.'

'Jon. Let's see. Great!' She ticks off my name and laughs. 'I know it feels strange on the first night, but don't be nervous – in a couple of weeks' time, this'll feel like home.'

I drift into the church. There are agnostics everywhere, eating shepherd's pie from paper plates on their laps. Michael Alison, one-time parliamentary private secretary to Mrs Thatcher, is here. So is an ex-England cricket captain. I spot the manager of a big British pop group. Samantha Fox found God through Nicky Gumbel, as did Geri Halliwell. I wonder whether Jonathan Aitken will pour the coffee, but he is nowhere to be seen tonight. And now Nicky Gumbel is on stage, leaning against the podium, smiling hesitantly. He reminds me of Tony Blair.

'A very warm welcome to you all. Now some of you may be thinking, "Help! What have I got myself into?"' A laugh. 'Don't worry,' he says. 'We're not going to pressurize you into doing anything. Perhaps some of you are sitting there sneering. If you are, please don't think that I'm looking down at you. I spent half my life as an atheist. I used to go to talks like this and I would sneer.'

Nicky is being disingenuous. We know there are no talks like this – Alpha is uniquely successful, and branching out abroad, so far to a hundred and twelve countries, where they play Nicky's videos and the pastor acts the part of Nicky. 'This just may be the wrong time for you,' says Nicky to the sneerers. 'If you don't want to come along next week, that's fine. Nobody will phone you up! I'd like you to meet Pippa, my wife.'

We applaud. 'Hi!' says Pippa. 'We've got three children. Henry is twenty, there's Jonathan, and Rebecca is fifteen.'

Nicky assures us that we are not abnormal for being here. The Bible is the world's most popular book, he says. This is normal. 'Forget the modern British novelists and the TV tie-ins,' he says, 'forty-four million Bibles are sold each year.' He says that the New Testament was written when they say it was. 'We know this very accurately,' he explains, 'through a science called textual criticism.' He says Jesus existed. This is historically verifiable. He quotes the Jewish historian Josephus, born AD 37: 'Jesus, a wise man, if it be lawful to call him a man, for he was a doer of wonderful works ... the tribe of Christians so named after him are not extinct to this day.' I am with Nicky thus far. My knowledge of Josephus is sketchy, but he strikes me as a reliable source. But the agnostics here – it soon becomes clear that Nicky can read our minds – are thinking, But none of this proves that Jesus was anything more than a human teacher.

Nicky tells an anecdote: he says that he once failed to recognize that his squash partner was Paul Ackford, the

England rugby international. Similarly, Jesus's disciples, in the region of Caesarea Philippi, failed to recognize that their master was the Son of God.

I could live without the squash anecdote.

Nicky says that Jesus could not have been just a great human teacher. When he was asked at his trial whether he was 'the Christ, the Son of the Living God, he replied: "I am."' Nicky's point is this: a great human teacher would not claim to be the Son of God.

'You must make your choice – either this man was, and is, the Son of God, or else he's a lunatic or, worse, the Devil of Hell. But don't let us come up with any patronizing nonsense about his being a great moral teacher. He hasn't left that open to us. He didn't intend to.'

This final logic (a quote from one of Nicky's heroes, C. S. Lewis) is impressive to me. It remains in my mind.

Then it's on to the small group. I am in Nicky's group: as is typical, it consists of around ten agnostics, some from the City, some professional sportspeople, strangers gathered together in a small room in the basement. We sit in a circle. I wonder what will happen to us in the weeks ahead. For now, we verbalize our doubts. We gang up on Nicky and his helpers: his wife, Pippa, an investment banker called James and his doctor wife, Julia, all ex-agnostics who found Christ on Alpha. We ask them antagonistic questions. 'If there's a God, why is there so much suffering?' And: 'What about those people who have never heard of Jesus? Are you saying that all other religions are damned?'

Nicky just smiles and says, 'What do the other people here think?'

At the end of the night, Nicky hands out some pamphlets he's written called (such is the predictability of agnostics) *Why Does God Allow Suffering?* (answer: nobody really knows) and *What About Other Religions?* (answer: they will, unfortunately, be denied entrance to the Kingdom of Heaven. This includes me – I am a Jew).

I am enjoying myself enormously. I drive away thinking about the things Nicky said. I play them over in my mind. But by the time I arrive home and then watch *ER*, my mini-epiphany has all drained away, and I go back to normal. I cannot imagine how any of my fellow agnostics will possibly be converted by the end of the course.

As the weeks progress, the timetable becomes routine. Dinner, a talk from Nicky, coffee and digestives, the small groups. But the hostile questions have now become slightly less combative. One agnostic, Alice, who is the financial manager of an Internet company and rides her horse every weekend in Somerset, admits to taking Nicky's pamphlets away with her on business trips. She says she reads them on the plane and finds them comforting. We talk about the excuses we give our friends for our weekly Wednesday night absences. Some say they're learning French. Others say they're on a business course. There is laughter and blushing. I miss Week Three because I am reporting on wife-swapping parties in Paris. On Week Four, Nicky suggests I tell the group all about wife swapping. The group asks me lots of questions. When I fill in the details, Nicky shakes his head mournfully. 'What about the children,' he sighs. 'So many people getting hurt.' He's right. Nicky ends the night by saying to me: 'I think it's important that you saw something awful like that midway through Alpha.'

Week Five, and Nicky is on stage talking about answered prayers and how coincidences can sometimes be messages from God. He says he keeps a prayer diary and ticks them off when they are answered. As Nicky says these things, I think about how my wife and I were told we couldn't have a baby. We went through fertility treatment for four years. Every month was like a funeral without a corpse. And then we did have a baby, and when Joel was born I thought of him as a gift from God.

The moment I think about this, I hear Nicky say the word 'Joel'. I look up. Nicky is quoting from the Book of Joel: 'I will repay you for the years the locusts have eaten.'

Later, I tell the group what happened. 'Ahhh,' they say, when I get to the part about us having a baby. 'Ahhh,' they say again, when I get to the part about Nicky saying Joel, and then reading out an uncannily appropriate quote.

'Well?' I say.

'I don't know,' Nicky smiles. 'I think you should let it sit in your heart and make your own decision.'

'But what do you think?' I say.

'If I had to put a bet on it,' he says, 'coincidence or message, I'd say definitely, yes, that was a message from God.'

The subject is changed.

'So?' says Nicky. 'How was everyone's week?'

Tony sits next to Alice. He is the most vociferous agnostic in the group. He always turns up in his business suit, straight from work, and has a hangdog expression, as if something is always troubling him.

'Tony?' says Nicky. 'How was your week?'

'I was talking to a homosexual friend,' says Tony, 'and he said that ever since he was a child he found himself attracted to other boys. So why does the Church think he's committing a sin? Are you damned if you commit a sexual act that is completely normal to you? That seems a bit unfair, doesn't it?'

There is a murmur of agreement from the group.

'First of all,' says Nicky, 'I have many wonderful homosexual friends. There's even an Alpha for gays running in Beverly Hills! Really! I think it's marvellous! But if a paedophile said, "Ever since I was a child I found myself attracted to children," we wouldn't say that that was normal, would we?'

A small gasp.

'Now, I am not for a moment comparing homosexuals with paedophiles,' Nicky continues, 'but the Bible makes it very clear that sex outside marriage, including homosexual sex, is, unfortunately, a sin.' He says he wishes it wasn't so, but the Bible makes it clear that gay people need to be healed.

'Although I strongly advise you not to say the word "healed" to them,' he quickly adds. 'They hate that word.'

The meeting is wound up. Nicky, Pippa and I stay around for a chat. We talk about who we feel might be on the cusp of converting. My money is on Alice.

'Really?' says Nicky. 'You think Alice?'

'Of course,' I say. 'Who do you think?'

'Tony,' says Nicky.

'Tony?' I say.

'We'll see,' says Nicky.

I drive home. In the middle of the night it becomes clear to me that I almost certainly had a message from

God – that God had spoken to me through Nicky Gumbel.

Woman leads church boycott in row over evangelical pig-snorting

A woman has walked out of her church and is holding services in her living room because she says she cannot bring herself to 'snort like a pig and bark like a dog' on a Church of England course. Angie Golding, 50, claims she was denied confirmation unless she signed up for the Alpha Course, which she says is a 'brainwashing' exercise where participants speak in tongues, make animal noises and then fall over. Mark Elsdon-Dew of HTB, Holy Trinity Brompton, said the Alpha Course included lectures on the Holy Spirit. 'It affects different people in different ways,' he said.

– The Times, 11 May 1996

Of course, stumbling upon this press cutting comes as a shock. I had no idea that the shepherd's pie, the nice chats, that these things seem to be leading up to something so peculiar; something that will, I guess, occur during our weekend away in Kidderminster.

I visit Mark Elsdon-Dew, Nicky's press man. I have grown fond of Mark. 'Do anything you want,' he frequently tells me. 'Go home, if you like. Really. Any time

you want. Don't worry, I won't phone you up! Ha ha!'
Mark was once the *Daily Express*'s news editor, but
then he did Alpha and now he works for Nicky, in a
Portakabin on HTB's two and a half acres. Nicky has so
many staff – more, even, than the Archbishop of Canterbury, says Mark – that there aren't enough offices in this
giant church to accommodate them all. I want to test
Mark, to see how honest he'll be about the negative
press. I ask him if any journalist has written disapprov-
ingly about Nicky. 'Oh, yes,' he says excitedly. 'Hang on,
let me find them for you.' Mark rifles through his filing
cabinets and retrieves a sheaf of articles. 'Look at this!'
he says. 'And how about this?' One article, from the
Spectator, suggests that Nicky's organization is akin to
Invasion of the Body Snatchers, something that looks
like the Anglican Church, acts like the Anglican Church,
but is something else, something malignant, growing,
poised to consume its host: 'For now they need the
Church of England for its buildings – but they are very
aware that through the wealth of their parishioners they
wield an influence over the established Church that far
outweighs their numbers.'

'If you think that's bad,' says Mark, 'you should see
this one.'

Oh, good, I think.

It reads: 'HTB's divorce from the real world, together

with a simplistic and communal response to all problems, a strong leader, and a money-conscious hierarchy, are trademarks of a cult.'

'And here's a real stinker,' says Mark.

'The Alpha Course: is it Bible-Based or Hell-Inspired?'

This last one is from the Reverend Ian Paisley. His conclusion, after fifteen pages of deliberation, is that it is Hell-Inspired.

Usually, when a discovery such as this presents itself midway through researching a story, I feel nothing but glee. On this occasion, however, the gaiety is tinged with indignation and relief – indignation that these people, this apparent cult, has managed to get under my skin, to instil in me feelings of some kind of awakening, and relief because I no longer feel the need to deal with those feelings.

It is Saturday morning in the countryside near Kidderminster, and Nicky is offering us the strangest invitation. He is going to beckon us into the supernatural, where he hopes we will physically feel the Holy Spirit enter our bodies. Nicky tells me that he very much hopes people will speak in tongues. 'I'm so glad you could make it,' he tells me.

'I'm glad to be here,' I say, although I am thinking, Are you a cult leader?

We've been arriving all night – in BMWs and Mercedes and Porsches – at the Pioneer Centre, a residential youth club booked for the weekend. The traffic was terrible. I was stuck in a jam behind a Minivan emblazoned with the words 'Jews For Jesus', and toyed with the idea of taking this to be another message from God, but I chose to discount it.

We are staying in dormitories – six to a room. Nicky and Pippa are not bunking up with the flock: Nicky says he needs space to concentrate. I don't think the agnostics quite grasp the reality of what will unfold in the next thirty-six hours. Many are completely unaware. Tongues!? How can Nicky make this happen?

The next morning, we laze in the sun and then we are called into the chapel, a big pine hut. Tonight, England will play Germany. Nicky takes to the stage: 'Now, some of you may be thinking, "Help! What's going to happen?" Well, first, I hope you have a wonderful time. Enjoy the weather, enjoy the sports, but, most of all, I hope we all experience the Holy Spirit.'

Nicky says that the Holy Spirit has often been ignored by the Church because it sounds 'weird and supernaturally evil'. He says the Church fears change, that he once said to an elderly vicar, 'You must have seen so many changes,' and that the vicar replied, 'Yes, and I have resisted every single one of them.' We laugh.

Nicky says that this is a shame, because when people open themselves to the Holy Spirit you can see it in their faces. 'Their faces are alive!' Look at Bach and Handel and da Vinci, he says. They had the Holy Spirit. Whatever line of work we're in – we could be bankers, 'or journalists' – we can be filled to overflowing. Nicky says that it is absolutely amazing. 'All relationships involve emotions. I don't say to Pippa, "I love you intellectually." What I say is, "I love you with my whole being, my mind, my heart, my will." Ah, but that's in private. The British don't display emotions in public, do they?' There is a silence. 'Just imagine,' he says, 'that England will score a goal tonight. I think some people will go, "Yeaah!"' There is more laughter. The audience is relaxed. 'If a comedy film makes us laugh out loud in the cinema, the movie is considered a success. If a tragic play makes us weep in a theatre, the play is considered a success. But if a religious service makes us weep or laugh, we are accused of emotionalism!'

And so it goes on, with Nicky managing to make the most alarming prospect seem acceptable. Speaking in tongues would normally be something absurd, horrific even. But imperceptibly, gracefully, Nicky is leading us there.

We have a few hours off. We swim and play basketball. The crowd is, as always, mainly white and wealthy.

A criticism levelled at Nicky by other Anglicans is that Jesus cast his net wide to embrace poor fishermen, whereas Nicky seems to concentrate on rich widows, Old Etonians and young high-fliers. This annoys him, far more than the accusations that he is a cult leader. He points out a group of men on the edge of the basketball court. They lean against a picket fence, watching the game with an inscrutable vigilance, huge and tanned, like a prison gang during their hour in the yard.

'You absolutely must meet Brian,' says Nicky. 'He's quite amazing.'

Brian is not his real name.

'I was a villain,' says Brian. 'A professional criminal.'

'Were you in a firm?' I ask.

'I *was* the firm,' he smiles. 'Say no more.'

From Brian's demeanour – he looks the archetypal English crime boss – I don't doubt this for a moment. It makes me smile: most vicars will proudly introduce you to some redeemed petty thief in their flock; once again Nicky attracts someone from the apex of his chosen profession. Back in the eighties, Brian was caught trying to pull off an enormous importation of cannabis. He was sentenced to ten years in jail. In 1994, while in Exeter Prison, Brian heard about Alpha. To curry favour with the chaplain, he called Nicky and asked him to visit the prison. Nicky sent a team instead.

'And within weeks,' says Brian, 'all these hard men were waving our arms around like we were in a night-club. Can you imagine it? People getting touched by the Holy Spirit, boys I knew who got banged up for some really naughty crimes . . .'

That was the first time a prison had run an Alpha Course. Brian was transferred to Dartmoor and took Alpha with him. Other converts did the same. That's how it spread through the prison system. Today, 120 of the 158 British prisons run Alpha Courses; some have six-month waiting lists.

Then there is this, from the March 2000 Alpha news-letter: 'US Governor George W Bush was so impressed by the impact of Alpha in the British prison system that he wants to start a trial programme at once in Texas.' 'And all that started with Brian in 1994,' says Nicky. 'It was such an amazing year.'

Indeed it was: on 20 January 1994, at a concrete church next to Toronto airport, eighty per cent of the congregation, apropos of nothing, suddenly fell to the floor and began writhing around, apparently singing in tongues and convulsing violently. Rumours about this milestone – which became known as the Toronto Blessing – quickly spread to Britain. Nicky flew to Toronto to see it for himself. Was it mass hysteria or a miracle, a real experience of the Holy Spirit?

'I don't talk about it now,' says Nicky. 'It divides people. It splits churches. It is very controversial. But I'll tell you – I think the Toronto Blessing was a wonderful, wonderful thing.'

Nicky returned from Canada, spoke passionately at HTB about the Toronto Blessing and, lo and behold, his congregation, too, began rolling on the floor, etc. The services soon became so popular, with queues around the block, they were compelled to introduce two Sunday-evening sittings – and still not everyone could get in. HTB became Britain's richest church. (It still is: last year's income was £5.1m.) This evangelical euphoria lasted the year, with miracles such as Prison Alpha cropping up all over the place. And then it ebbed away.

But its influence has lasted. The Toronto Blessing was the kick-start Alpha needed. Alpha began at HTB in 1979, as a brush-up course for rusty churchgoers. Hardly anybody attended. It trundled along, causing no ripples, until Nicky arrived in 1991. Nicky is the son of agnostics. He discovered God while studying for the Bar at Cambridge, and gave up a career as a barrister to be ordained into the C of E in 1986. He saw Alpha's potential. What if he began targeting agnostics? What if he gave it an image makeover?

'Nicky bought standard lamps back in 1991,' says Mark later that afternoon. 'He took an interest in the food. There are flowers. Young, quite pretty girls welcome you at the door. Nicky identified some very important things. First, informality. Second, the course – people like the idea of going on a course, whether it's yoga or Christianity. Third, free and easy – we don't force anything down people's throats. People have a horror of being phoned up. And, finally, boredom – we will not bore you.'

Nicky's new direction combined with his charisma, his dazzlingly constructed weekly talks chipping away at our doubts and the Toronto Blessing caused Alpha's popularity to explode through the nineties. In 1992, there were five Alpha Courses in Britain; 100 rusty churchgoers attended that year. By 1994 there were 26,700 attendees. By the end of last year, there were 14,200 courses around the world, with 1.5 million attendees. Nicky has sold more than a million books.

Alice had a wedding to go to, but hopes to arrive by this evening. The rest of our group gathers on the grass. We talk about our feelings about the Holy Spirit.

'I've got to say,' says a woman called Annie, 'the idea of speaking in tongues really freaks me out.'

Nicky nods and smiles.

'I agree,' says Jeremy, who works with asylum-seekers. 'I really don't want to be seen as some kind of freak.'

'You won't suddenly become weirdos,' explains James's

one of the group leaders. 'You won't lose your sense of humour, or your mates or whether you drink beer or not.'

'We shouldn't get too hung up on tongues,' adds Julia, James's wife, and a fellow group leader. 'Tongues is just one of the many gifts. Tony? What do you think?'

Tony lights a cigarette. 'Do you have to believe in God before you receive the gift?' he says. 'Because it seems strange to ask someone you don't believe in to prove that he exists.'

I wonder what makes Nicky think that Tony is our group's best candidate for conversion.

'The Church likes to put God in a box,' says James. 'The Church wants to make God safe. We think the Church has lost the plot. We just want God to be God. As the Apostle Paul said, "I would that you all speak in tongues."'

We ask if they can speak in tongues, and they all say they can. James has been speaking in tongues for several years. Julia was fearful at first, but now does it a lot. Nicky and Pippa are extremely well versed in tongues, which, they say, literally means 'languages never learnt'.

They say that on countless occasions they have heard people who can't speak Chinese, for instance, speaking in Chinese tongues. Such miracles appear to be commonplace once one enters the arena of tongues – as we will do at around 6.30 p.m. tonight.

At 6 p.m., we are back in the chapel. Nicky is on stage, telling us nothing bad will happen to us.

'You don't need to speak in tongues. It is not the most important gift. But tongues is a beginner's gift, and Alpha is a beginner's course in Christianity, so it would be wonderful if you tried.' We steel ourselves. The door opens. It is Alice. She has missed Nicky's comforting preamble and has arrived just in time for the main event.

'If you ask for the Holy Spirit, you're not going to get something terrible,' says Nicky. 'Shall we give it a try? Shall we ask Him?'

'Mmm,' say the crowd, contentedly.

Nicky softly begins: 'Please stand up and close your eyes. If there's anyone who would like to experience the Holy Spirit, maybe you're not sure, I'd like you to say a very simple prayer in your heart . . . a very simple prayer . . . It's OK . . . I now turn from everything that is wrong . . . now hold out your hands . . . hold them out in front of you . . . if you'd like to . . . some of you might be experiencing a weight on your hands . . . you might be thinking nothing's happening . . . but you might be feeling a peace . . . a deep peace . . . that, too, is a manifestation of the Holy Spirit . . . Jesus is telling you He loves you . . . He died for you.'

This is when the first sob comes – at the front, some-one begins to cry. 'I sense that some of you would like to receive the gift of tongues now.'

I wobble on my feet. Later, James tells me that wobbling is a possible sign of the Holy Spirit. I open my eyes for a moment and look at the group. Tony is grinning, his eyes bulging, like a schoolboy in a pompous assembly. Alice, who is entirely unprepared, is looking perplexed and uncomfortable. I close my eyes. I imagine those who have been in this spell before me, Jonathan Aitken, for instance, and the business executives and celebrities.

'Start to praise God in any language but the language you speak . . . Don't worry about your neighbour. Your neighbour will be worried enough about himself . . .'

And then the tongues begin. I thought it would be cacophonous, but it turns out to be haunting, tuneful, like some experimental opera.

I think some people are cheating – I hear French: 'C'est oui. C'est oui' – but mostly it is quite beautiful. I open my eyes again and look around. Mark, Nicky's press officer, is speaking in tongues. So are James and Julia. All these people I have known all these weeks are speaking in tongues. Tony has refrained from tongues, but he is no longer grinning, either. He is crying. Alice looks ready to explode with anger. She barges out of the chapel.

'Be a little bolder now . . .' Nicky carries on. 'Just continue to receive this wonderful opportunity . . .'

James walks over to me: 'Is it working for you?' he asks.

'Well, it might have,' I reply, 'but the truth is, I'm a journalist, so I couldn't keep my eyes closed.'

'Would you like me to pray for you?' he asks.

'OK,' I say.

James rests his hand on my shoulder. 'O Jesus, I pray that Jon will receive Your wonderful spirit. God. Please come and fill Jon with . . .'

It is not working. The spell has broken. I tell James again that I'm sorry, but I'm a journalist. (This is no excuse – the picture editor of a Sunday newspaper is speaking in tongues to my left, as is a producer of Channel 4 documentaries in front of me, for the first time in his life.) So James changes tack. 'Oh thank you, Jesus, for Jon's wonderfully enquiring journalistic mind . . . please help Jon's career . . . no, not his career . . . his wonderful journalism . . . and may his journalism become even more wonderful now he is working in Your name, Jesus Christ . . .'

I tell James I'm sorry, and follow Alice outside, where

Jon Ronson

half a dozen furious agnostics have gathered on the grass. 'Why didn't anyone tell me I'd signed up for a brainwashing cult?' says one. 'I felt like I was in a pack of hyenas. I wanted someone to come up and ask me if I was OK, and instead someone came up and said, "Would you like me to pray for you?"'

Alice is devastated: 'I used to think Nicky was fantastic. He really gave me room to investigate my feelings about the Lord. But now I'm thinking, just get me away from these weirdos. I've been dragged all the way out here under false pretences, and there's no escape. I am actually very, very upset.'

We turn out to be in the minority, and watch as the new converts file out of the chapel, red-eyed from crying or smiling beatifically. Tony is one such convert, but he is not smiling. In fact, he seems miserable. 'Something overwhelmed me,' he says. 'I didn't want it to. I tried to resist it, but I couldn't.'

'What was it?' I ask.

'The Holy Spirit,' says Tony.

'What did it feel like?'

'Like when you're trying not to cry but you can't help yourself. I was thinking of all the reasons why I didn't want it to happen – you know, the Christian lifestyle – and then Nicky came over to me and started whispering in my ear.'

'What did he say?'

'He said, "I sense that you have had a Christian experience in the past." And that rocked my world, because I have, and I didn't tell anyone. That's why I came on Alpha. I wanted to decide, once and for all, yes or no. And . . .' Tony sighs discontentedly. 'God spoke to me just now. He said, "You can come back."'

Back in London the next Wednesday, Nicky's topic is 'Spiritual Warfare: How Can I Resist The Devil?'. He says that the Devil's tricks include planting doubts – I wonder if he is referring to those people, such as Alice and me, who doubted the power of tongues. Then I think, maybe the Devil really is planting doubts in my mind. I am becoming increasingly anti-Nicky. Is Satan working within me? I conclude that I have been on this story for a long time and perhaps need a few weeks off. Nicky turns up the heat. He says we must not take an unhealthy interest in horror movies, Ouija boards, palmists, healers and so on. These are the Devil's tools.

Later, in the small group, a woman called Suzanne asks a question. She didn't speak in tongues in Kidderminster but she did burst into tears. 'I went to a clairvoyant a few weeks ago,' says Suzanne. 'That surely can't be a sin.'

'I'm afraid it is,' says Nicky.

'Really?'

'I would actually ask God for forgiveness for that,' says Nicky.

'Oh, come on,' snorts Suzanne. 'Where does the Bible say that?'

'Deuteronomy,' says Nicky.

'Oh,' says Suzanne.

'Poor Suzanne,' whispers Alice to me, 'being made to feel guilty about going to some silly clairvoyant.'

The atmosphere has changed.

'Things are coming to the boil,' says Alice. 'Can't you feel the screws being tightened?'

'How are you feeling?' I ask her.

'Judged,' she says.

Annie is no longer freaked out about speaking in tongues. She feels instead that she experienced God's love in Kidderminster. 'It was the most beautiful experience of my life,' she says. At first, she hated it, but now she realizes that her perception was wrong and that the tongue-speakers are the lucky ones. Annie can now speak in tongues.

Nicky asks Tony to tell the group what happened to him in Kidderminster, but he quietly replies, 'No comment.'

Then Alice confronts Nicky. She tells him she felt trapped in Kidderminster. 'It was group pressure. I am very, very upset. I know that you're looking at me like I'm a failure.'

Nicky smiles: 'Nothing could be further from the truth. We simply want to create a non-threatening, non-judgemental environment.'

'Judged is what I feel,' says Alice.

'Then we have failed,' says Nicky.

Later that night, Nicky holds me back for a moment. I think he's concerned about how I responded to the tongues. After my Joel mini-testimony, I presume he hoped that I, too, would speak in them.

'Some journalists miss the story,' says Nicky. 'Lots of journalists miss the story. But you haven't. You've got the story. I knew it from the beginning.'

'What is the story?' I ask Nicky.

'That something amazing is happening,' he says. 'Something incredible. All over the world. In a hundred and sixteen countries.'

'I thought it was a hundred and twelve countries,' I say.

'That was a month ago,' says Nicky. 'Now it's a hundred and sixteen countries.' We laugh. 'I would feel absolutely awful about Alice,' he says, 'but I feel completely free from responsibility.'

'Do you?' I ask.

'I'm not hypnotizing anybody,' he says. 'I don't know anything about hypnosis.'

It is getting late. Tomorrow is the start of the Alpha international conference. There will be much good news to report. Alpha is up 156 per cent in New Zealand; one-third of all churches there now run the course. My personal experience with Alpha finishes here. I miss the last few weeks because I have to travel to America. In my group, of those who lasted the course, about 70 per cent were won over.

Alice leaves some messages on my answerphone. She says I have missed some incredible things. I call her and ask what happened.

'It was just amazing,' she says. 'Nicky did a session on healing.'

'Healing?'

'Healing by prayer. He started saying, "I sense someone here has a lump on their left breast that they're very concerned about." There were maybe twenty-five of these, and he got it right every time. People were standing up and everyone prayed for them. And then I asked them to pray for my horse, who's ill, and the horse got better. And I had a terrible pain in my left side and I didn't mention it, but Nicky said he sensed it and everyone prayed for me and now the pain is gone.'

'Wow,' I say.

'Nicky was gutted that you missed it,' says Alice.

'You sound like you've changed your mind again,' I say.

'Oh, I don't know,' says Alice. 'All I can say is that my horse got better and the pain has gone from my left side.' She pauses. 'For all my problems with Kidderminster, I've got to say that Nicky is quite brilliant. He's wonderful.'

And I have to admit that, for all my problems with Kidderminster, I can only agree with her.

4. THE FRANK SIDEBOTTOM YEARS

For three years, in the late eighties, I was the keyboard player with the Frank Sidebottom Oh Blimey Big Band. Frank wore a big papier-mâché head, the act involved doing oompah versions of pop classics, and those were his zenith years. We toured the country, playing to sell-out crowds in medium-sized venues. We rode high. And then it all went wrong.

Now, fifteen years after I last spoke to Frank, I receive an email out of the blue: 'There's an 8 foot mosaic of the Oh Blimey Big Band going up in the Tate Gallery next month. You know it is, it really is, thank you.'

Could that really be Frank? I think. 'Frank?' I email back. 'Is that you?'

In 1987, when I was twenty, my job was to put on concerts for the Polytechnic of Central London. I became friendly over the phone with an agent from Cheshire called Mike Doherty. He looked after Ronnie Corbett, but his true calling was being Frank Sidebottom's drummer.

One day Mike phoned me in a panic and said, 'Frank's playing a show in London tonight and our keyboard player can't make it. Do you know any keyboard players?'

'I can play the keyboards,' I replied.

'Well, *you're in*!' he shouted.

'But I don't know any of the songs,' I said.

'Can you play C, F and G?' he asked.

'Yes,' I said.

'Well, *you're in*!' he shouted.

I arrived at the venue: the Cricketers' in South London. Frank was preparing to sound-check. Even though the concert was a few hours away, he was already wearing the papier-mâché head: two wide bug eyes staring, a mouth frozen into a half-smile, red lips slightly parted, as if mildly surprised, very flat hair, a permanent tan, there in the dingy half-light of this empty pub. He was fiddling with some equipment. Why was he wearing the head when there was nobody to see it except the band and the pub landlord? Did he wear it *all* the time, like Michael Redgrave with the ventriloquist dummy in *Dead of Night*? Close up, the head was bumpy. (Later, in the early 1990s, he made a far smoother fibreglass version.) I knew his real name was Chris, so I approached and said, 'Hello, Chris. I'm Jon.'

He ignored me.

'Hello, Chris,' I said again.

He continued to ignore me.

'Hello, uh, Frank?' I tried.

'*Hello!*' he yelled.

Mike the drummer came over to explain that when Chris puts on the head, Chris ceases to be. And sure enough, during the years that followed, I never heard him respond to the name Chris while dressed as Frank. I discovered why he was in the head hours before the show: he'd been doing a public event at a record shop earlier that afternoon, and his habit – in situations like that – was to just stay being Frank.

'We'll put you over here,' said Mike, setting up a keyboard stand for me at the side of the stage. Frank gave me a quick lesson. The songs were, indeed, comprised entirely of C, F and G. They were all covers – 'I Should Be So Lucky', 'Material Girl', 'Every Breath You Take' – so I picked it up quite quickly. And then the audience arrived. And – I can say this because this was Frank's vision, and I was just a session musician, just an oily rag – it was brilliant. There was something fantastically warped about the act, which was four men assiduously emulating and fleshing out with real instruments the swing-beat chord sound of a cheap children's Casio keyboard, with a living, slightly eerie cartoon character prancing around at the front, singing in a nasal Mancunian twang, as if he had a swimming peg attached to his nose. Each song ended with the same words: 'You know it is, it really is, thank you.'

As we played that night, to a room packed with hundreds of euphoric people including Midge Ure, I marvelled at the train of creative thought that had somehow led to this bizarre and unique place.

At the end of the show Frank introduced the band. 'On guitar, Rick Sarko!' The audience cheered. 'On drums, Mike Doherty!' The audience cheered. 'On keyboards, Jon Ronson.' Nobody cheered.

What's gone wrong? I thought. And then I realized. Concerned that I didn't know any of the songs, they had turned my keyboard right down and positioned my stand so far behind the speaker stack that – unbeknownst to me until that moment – the majority of the audience had no idea I was there.

Why did they even bother asking me? I thought miserably on the journey home. And then, a few weeks later, Mike called and asked if I wanted to join the band full time, and so I moved to Manchester.

In those days, the identity of the man under the head was the subject of great speculation. On many occasions,

Sidebottom fans would barge into the dressing room before a show and refuse to leave until the real Frank revealed himself. They'd go around the room: 'It's you, isn't it? No. *You're* Frank, aren't you?'

On most occasions, the only person they wouldn't bother asking was the unassuming Chris, who blended into the wall.

By 1987, Frank Sidebottom had existed for three years. Chris had previously been in a Manchester punk band called The Freshies. They had one minor hit – 'I'm In Love With A Girl On A Manchester Virgin Megastore Checkout Desk' – but that was all. Chris, at a loose end, sketched the character of Frank, recorded a terrible version of 'Anarchy in the UK' with Casio accompaniment and sent it around the major record labels with a covering letter that began, 'Dear—, I'm thinking of getting into showbusiness. Do you have any pamphlets?'

Someone at EMI found it funny enough to invite him in. He arrived, dressed as Frank, and as he walked in the A&R man asked, 'Have you been in showbusiness for long?'

Frank looked at his watch and replied, 'Ten seconds.'

His debut EP, released on EMI, was called *Frank's Firm Favourites*. The comedy came from the juxtaposition of the parochialism of Frank's everyday suburban life and the grandiosity of the songs he covered. In real life, Frank's life was much like Chris's. Both lived in an unremarkable cul-de-sac in Timperley, Cheshire. Biographical details were revealed in songs like 'Born in Timperley' (to the tune of 'Born in the USA'): 'I go shopping in Timperley/They've got loads of shops/That's where I do the shopping for my mum/Five pounds of potatoes and loads of chops.'

Chris invented a cast of supporting characters, who would pop up between the songs on his radio show, *Radio Timperley*. There was the puppet, Little Frank. There was the neighbour, Mrs Merton. Chris asked his brother-in-law's friend, the then BBC secretary Caroline Aherne, to do the voice of Mrs Merton, which is how she came to exist.

Paying close attention to Frank's burgeoning world was Graham Fellows, who went on to invent John Shuttleworth on Sidebottom principles, and eventually became more famous, a little like Nirvana did with the Pixies.

(I think Chris was, understandably, a little embittered by Mrs Merton and John Shuttleworth's subsequent successes.)

Frank's Firm Favourites charted at about number 90. EMI dropped him. But by then his following was sufficiently large to pay me £40 a night to be his keyboard player. And I did, for two happy years, becoming his booking agent too.

Frank supported Bros at Wembley, and Gary Glitter at a Freshers' Ball somewhere. Glitter's roadies were extremely rude from the beginning, cornering the band and issuing a stringent list of dos and don'ts: 'You aren't allowed to use our lights. Stay away from our hydraulic stage.' And so on.

Under the head, Chris was seething.

And so, as soon as Frank went on, he jumped onto the hydraulic floor, which set off smoke bombs and rose dramatically above the heads of the audience.

'Come on! Come on!' sang Frank. 'Do you want to be in my gang?' Within twenty seconds he spotted Gary Glitter's roadies pushing their way through the audience towards him. He jumped offstage and ran down the corridor, pulling off his head and costume as he went – he had his own clothes underneath – just as the roadies caught up with him.

'Did you see Frank Sidebottom?' they asked him.

'He went that way,' said Chris.

We were riding high. And then it all went wrong. Chris announced he was going to make the band more professional-sounding. He hired a proper saxophone player, and an overly suave bass player called Richard. Richard played in an effeminate Manchester guitar band, but there was nothing effeminate about him. He took an instant dislike to me and – two rehearsals in – threatened to take me outside and 'break' my 'keyboard-playing fingers'.

Suddenly, we were rehearsing a lot more than we used to. We were building virtuoso sax and guitar solos into 'Timperley Sunset' and 'Anarchy in Timperley'. I don't want to sound wise after the fact, but it was clear to me that this was heading for disaster, and only I had the foresight to realize it.

'The audience don't want a note-perfect Oh Blimey Big Band,' I urgently told Mike the drummer one day during a break from rehearsals.

'Yes,' Mike replied. 'But we can't just spend our lives sounding bobbins. We need to move it forward.'

(Bobbins was, by the way, a word popularized by Frank. It may end up being his most enduring legacy.)

'The audience isn't going to like it,' I warned.

I booked Frank a huge thirty-date tour. It was decided in rehearsals that I'd begin the show. I'd walk on, alone, into the spotlight, and play a powerful C. This lone note would last a minute or more, a simple but compellingly forceful C pulsating through the venue. It would ignite the audience into a frenzy of anticipation. Then the rest of the band would join me and we'd open by thrashing out a power-rock version of 'Born in Timperley'. The audience was noticeably perplexed. Where had our beloved sound gone? What were we thinking? We sounded like John Shuttleworth being backed by Survivor.

A few days into the tour we got an extremely caustic review in the *NME*. Previously they had always liked us. Now they expressed astonishment at our new musical direction. Word got around that we had lost our talent. By mid-tour, our audiences had dwindled from five hundred or so to thirty if we were lucky. Chris always said that his favourite shows were the ones where everything went wrong. There were lots of those in the latter half of the tour. In Dudley, there can't have been more than fifteen people in the audience. Midway through someone produced a ball. The audience split into two teams and, ignoring us, played a game. Richard the suave bass player was mortified at the lack of respect shown to our music. As we came offstage that night, Chris took off the head and said, 'That was the best show ever.'

When the tour ended, I lost contact with Chris and Mike. I moved back to London. I heard a rumour that Chris had got into trouble with the Inland Revenue.

Apparently, when the judge asked him how he'd like to pay his arrears he stood up and said, 'Would a pound a week suffice, m'lud?'

'No, it would not!' the judge yelled.

Fifteen years passed. Chris wound down Frank. He didn't retire him completely – there were solo shows, a greatest-hits CD – but Chris found a new way to earn a living: as an animator on *Pingu*. And then, out of the blue, I got the email about the eight-foot mosaic, and then another email with a photograph of it. It was created by the artist Mark Kennedy. It really was going up in Tate Britain, for one day only, the next day – 2 June. Frank would be there too, performing a solo show. A Tate curator, Andrew Shaw, is a big Frank fan, which is how this strange booking came to be.

There, in the mosaic, is the Radio 2 presenter Mark Radcliffe, wearing a fez. He was the keyboard player who couldn't make the London show, providing the vacancy for me. (He later rejoined the band on accordion.) There I am in the fez next to him. There's Mrs Merton. And there's Chris Evans with a steering wheel. This represents the fact that he was briefly, before he became famous, our driver. We used to tour around in a Transit van. One time we were playing in London. We pulled up on the Edgware Road. Chris Evans wound down the window and said the funniest thing I've ever heard.

'Excuse me?' he said.

'Yes?' said a passer-by.

'Is this London?' he said.

There was a silence.

'Yes,' said the passer-by.

'Well, where do you want this wood?' he said.

And there is Frank. Time hasn't ravaged him. He looks exactly the same.

He is planning a full comeback. My hope is that he'll ask me to play keyboards.

5. OUT OF THE ORDINARY

Friday, 10 September 2004

Before we go to bed my wife Elaine and I shout for our cat in a cheerfully high-pitched and carefree fashion. I stand at the back door. Elaine stands at the front.

'Monty!' we shout. 'Monty! Monty! Monty!'

I've always assumed that the neighbours, if they happen to overhear, would find it enchanting. What could be lovelier than the faraway call of someone summoning their cat? But tonight something disturbing happens.

'Monty!' I shout.

There is a silence.

'Monty!' someone apes, mockingly, in the darkness nearby.

I pause, startled.

'Someone just mocked me,' I say.

'What?' says Elaine.

'Shhh. Listen,' I say. *'Monty!'*

I adopt a more mannish, ominous tone, but it comes across as panicky.

'Monty!' calls back the anonymous mocker.

'It's probably just kids,' says Elaine. She is shaken too.

I wish it were true – kids or passing drunks. But this is the voice of a sober adult. It is an adult standing still, in his own home or garden, very close by. I realize that someone must have long harboured a secret loathing of me and can contain himself no longer: it has exploded out of him in the form of aping my voice. I realize too I will never again be able to call for Monty in an unselfconscious fashion. I don't want to sound over-dramatic but I feel like Adam in *Paradise Lost*: 'Cover me, ye Pines! Ye Cedars, with innumerable boughs Hide me.'

Monday, 20 September 2004

Disney World, Florida.

Joel has fallen for Mickey Mouse. Now he wants me to buy him Pal Mickey.

'Twenty dollars and it's just junk,' I say, picking it up in the shop. 'It's just a cuddly toy.'

I squeeze Pal Mickey's stomach: 'Say, pal, what did the sardine say when he saw the submarine? Look! A can of people! Ha ha gosh!'

'I see you've found Pal Mickey,' says a voice in my ear. I jump. The shopkeeper has crept up behind us. 'Pal Mickey knows where you are and he tells you things,' he says.

'Like what?' I ask.

'Well,' he says, 'if you're at the Magic Kingdom and there's no queue for Splash Mountain, Pal Mickey will let you know.'

'Pal Mickey will *know* when we're at the Magic Kingdom?' I ask. 'How will he know?'

'Satellite tracking technology,' says the shopkeeper.

'Wow,' says Joel.

'Does Pal Mickey know we're in this shop now?' I ask, staring at it with renewed apprehension.

There is a silence.

'Yes,' says the shopkeeper.

I buy Pal Mickey. We head off to Epcot.

'Pal Mickey will tell us what to do,' says Joel, confidently.

We stare at Pal Mickey. He says nothing. I wave him about at the sky. Still nothing. And then, suddenly: '*Gosh!*' yells Pal Mickey. Joel and I jump out of our skins. 'There's no line at Mission Space,' says Pal Mickey.

'*Let's go there now!*' says Joel.

It is 11 p.m., back at the hotel. Joel is drifting off to sleep with Pal Mickey in his arms. Suddenly, Pal Mickey yells: '*Gosh!*'

'Aargh!' screams Joel.

'Jesus,' I say.

'There's no line at Space Mountain,' says Pal Mickey.

'What's happening?' says Elaine.

'Pal Mickey is malfunctioning!' I yell. 'He thinks we're still at the Magic Kingdom.'

'*Turn him off!*' yells Elaine.

'Let's go to Space Mountain,' says Joel.

Tuesday, 21 September 2004

I am on a jam-packed Disney World courtesy bus, somewhere between Epcot and the Magic Kingdom. Joel has a Mickey Mouse basketball on his lap. He's distractedly practising martial arts on Mickey's face.

'Joel,' I joke, quite loudly, because I think it's funny and I want other people to overhear, 'when you hit Mickey's face, Mickey cries.'

'Mmm?' says Joel.

'When you hit Mickey's face, Mickey cries,' I repeat, grinning.

'What are you talking about?' asks Joel.

The people next to us on the bus have stopped talking and are also looking to me for an explanation.

'It's just a stupid joke,' says Elaine to Joel.

'Explain exactly what you *mean*,' says Joel. 'Where is Mickey crying?'

'Just *leave* it,' I hiss to Joel.

'Is Mickey Mouse crying?' Joel asks the bus in general. People tut.

'No,' someone tells him, soothingly.

Wednesday, 22 September 2004

North Florida. Elaine and Joel have gone back to London and I've stayed on for a few days do to some interviews here and in New York. I'm interviewing a group of anti-globalization protestors in a cafe. I offer to buy drinks. One asks for a peppermint tea, a few for chamomile.

'Oh, you communists!' I say. 'I know why you all drink herbal tea.'

'Why?' they ask.

'Because proper tea is theft!' I say.

They all roar with laughter. None of them have heard

this joke before and they think it is the funniest thing ever.

As I drive away, I am pulled over by the police. Still on a high from the success of the joke, I jump merrily out of the car to greet him.

'Freeze!' he yells, drawing his gun. 'Get back in your car *now*!'

I call home and tell Elaine and Joel what happened. We laugh about it.

Thursday, 23 September 2004

Joel phones and says he told everyone in class about the policeman yelling 'Freeze!' and pulling out his gun.

'Everyone laughed,' he says. He is thrilled. 'Even the teacher.'

'Really?' I say, also thrilled. 'The teacher too?'

'Everyone!' he says.

It was almost worth getting shot for this. These are the moments I will remember on my deathbed.

Saturday, 25 September 2004

I'm standing in Barnes and Noble, in Manhattan. It has been drummed into me by my publisher that whenever I am in a bookshop I should introduce myself to the customer-service people, say something engaging and offer to sign copies of my book. But I never do this. It seems rife with danger, although I cannot pinpoint exactly what the danger might be. Today, though, I am pleased to see that they have a small stack of my book *Them* on the 'Quirky and Interesting' table at the front.

These people must really like me! I think.

I watch a man in a baseball cap pick up a copy of it, read the dust jacket, put it down again and walk off.

What's your big problem? I think.

Still, I am very glad to see *Them* on display so I decide, I'm going to do it! I'm going to introduce myself to the customer-service people!

I walk to the customer-service table.

'Hello!' I say. 'I wrote *Them*.'

I wave my hand in the direction of the Quirky and Interesting table. She gives me a look.

'I just wanted to thank you for having *Them* on the front table,' I say, 'and if you would like me to sign any copies I will.'

'I'm sorry?' she says.

'I'm Jon Ronson,' I say, suddenly less sure of myself. Why is she looking at me funny? 'I, uh, wrote *Them*.'

Again, I wave my hand in the direction of the book.

'Them,' I say, pointing. 'I wrote *Them*. Do you want me to sign them?'

'That won't be necessary,' she says.

And then, suddenly, it hits me. To her eyes I am a man in a bookshop claiming to have written everything on the Quirky and Interesting table.

Oh Jesus, I think.

And I walk briskly out of the shop.

Saturday, 2 October 2004

I call my mother to tell her I'm in *Word* magazine.

'You want the new issue, not the one with Ry Cooder on the cover.'

'Who's Ry Cooder?' she asks.

'He's a guitarist,' I say.

'I've never heard of him,' she says.

'That doesn't mean he isn't somebody worth having heard of,' I snap. 'He did the music for *Paris, Texas*.'

'Why the sudden interest in Ry Cooder?' she snaps back.

'Why are you being so dismissive of Ry Cooder?' I counter. 'Anyway, you're looking for the magazine with Paul Weller on the cover.'

'Who's Paul Weller?' she asks.

'He's only one of the greatest musicians *ever*!' I declare, triumphantly.

'I don't believe I've ever heard you mention Ry Cooder *or* Paul Weller in your entire life,' she says.

'Well, they're both brilliant,' I say. 'They're both legendary. And they both absolutely deserve to be on the cover of a magazine. Ry Cooder pretty much re-invented the slide-guitar style' – I am almost screeching now – 'and Paul Weller has *legions* of fans and was a great mod punk singer who turned to soul later in his career, pretty much re-inventing all those genres. I can't *believe* you're being so cruel about Ry Cooder and Paul Weller,' I add, exasperatedly. 'It is completely gratuitous cruelty. If Paul Weller is so insignificant then why did Peter Blake, the man who did the *Sergeant Pepper* cover, design the cover for his album *Stanley Road*?'

'I've heard of the Beatles,' she says.

'Well, I'm sorry I'm not as successful as the Beatles,' I yell.

There is a silence.

'What are you talking about?' she asks.

*

81

Our neighbour is having a party. At midnight he flings open his patio doors and starts playing salsa music very loudly.

'That's it!' I say.

I get out of bed and march next door. I yell. I mention 'community spirit' and I use bad language. He turns the music off. Ten minutes later, I lie in bed and I can hear him through the walls. He's telling his guests a story. I can't make out the words but I hear the punchline. It is: 'Monty! Monty!'

Wednesday, 27 October 2004

Half term. It is only when we reach the front of the queue for the bungee trampoline, and my son has been harnessed up by the man wearing the Bungee Crew sweatshirt, do I realize there are two bungee trampolines, but only one Bungee Crewman.

Have they thought this through? I think.

The last time Joel was on one of these, at Thorpe Park, he had his own harness-puller. If he now has to share with the little blonde girl who's being harnessed up next to him whilst shouting, 'I can't wait! I can't wait!' it's clear what's going to happen. The wires, if not pulled after every bounce, will lose their elasticity and the unattended child will be left stranded midair.

But then I think, The man's a professional. The two trampolines are only a few feet apart. He'll pull the girl, like he's doing now, then he'll leap over to Joel, get him bouncing, and then back and forth. Any second now he'll attend to Joel.

The girl is shrieking with happiness. Joel, on the other hand, is like a parachutist caught in a tree, his legs dangling limply four feet from the ground. He gamely attempts a bounce but the physics are against him.

'This is boring,' he calls.

He's clearly favouring the girl, I think. He's brazenly favouring her.

He hops indifferently over to Joel, gives him a cursory pull, leaps excitedly back to the girl, and tugs her joyfully. It's like some fucking popularity contest. He obviously thinks Joel is sullen whereas the girl is enchanting, and is consequently more deserving of his energies. But this is twisted logic on his part, because it's his inattention that's causing my son's curmudgeonly attitude.

'Say something to him,' calls Joel, despondently, from his static position four feet from the ground.

I cough. 'Excuse me,' I say. 'Would you mind if I pull my son?'

'There's a technique,' the man mutters.

'Please pull me, Dad,' calls Joel.

I stare at the barrier but I am frozen to the spot. But then I think, No! I am *not* going to allow my child to be stigmatized by this. I'm *not* going to stand there and watch him be bullied by some thug in a Bungee Crew sweatshirt. And so I do it. My heart pounding, I step over the barrier.

When I think back on what happens next, it is as if it is in slow motion.

'There's a technique,' I hear the man growl, but I ignore him.

And I see he does nothing to stop me. I leap onto the trampoline and tug defiantly at my son's leg.

'Ow,' says Joel.

Then I tug some more and yes, he begins to bounce, higher and higher. 'Hooray!' says Joel. 'Thank you, Dad!'

'Let's *go*,' I say, proudly, 'to the dodgems!'

Then I say, to the Bungee Crewman, 'Excuse me, could you help me unharness my son?'

Friday, 26 November 2004

We are having lunch in a children's restaurant. A magician is going from table to table. She reaches us, and performs an amazing illusion in which she somehow pushes 10p through the glass of our empty bottle of water. The three of us applaud, astonished.

'I've just got time for one last trick,' she says.

She turns away to retrieve some cards from her bag, and as she does Elaine mouths at me, 'Give her a tip.'

I look startled and quickly shake my head no.

The magician turns back to us.

'Think of a card,' she says to Joel. 'Whisper it to your dad. Now I'm turning my head away so there's no way I'll be able to see what you're whispering.' She does.

'Seven of diamonds,' whispers Joel.

'*Tip her*,' Elaine frantically mouths at me.

'*I'm not sure she's expecting a tip*,' I frantically mouth back.

'And now . . .' says the magician, turning back.

Yes, she is standing over our restaurant table, which is a usual tipping scenario. But if I tip her aren't I effectively saying, 'You were superior to us while you were amazing us, but now it is over and here is a reminder that you were basically just serving us'?

'Is this your card?' she says.

I am so consumed with panic I've missed the trick.

Elaine pointedly glares at me, and then at my pocket. I take £2 out and I clumsily murmur, 'This is for you.'

She looks slightly hurt and confused.

Finally my nightmare has come true, I think. I have tipped someone who doesn't want to be tipped.

Later Elaine says, 'She only looked hurt because you tipped her awkwardly.'

Sunday, 28 November 2004

Our neighbour announces he's having a party, so we go away for the night, to a canal-side hotel near Watford. On Sunday morning, we go for a walk. A cyclist passes us on the towpath. I wave her a cheery good morning. She smiles and waves back, loses control and cycles straight into the canal.

Jesus, I think.

Elaine rushes towards the water. I make the instant decision to stand by Joel, my arm on his shoulder, my thought process being that as Joel has never seen anyone fall into a canal before, perhaps it might trigger off in his behaviour some unexpected turn of events that would end with *him* falling into the canal. I'm not entirely sure what that turn of events might be. Maybe he'll start running around in ever-increasing circles. This is unlikely, but who knows?

The woman in the canal looks traumatized.

'Grab my arm,' says Elaine.

A passer-by rushes to help, shooting me a glance that I suspect means 'Why aren't *you* helping?'

This, I think, must be the first time that something bad has happened in the countryside, in close proximity to me, that isn't directly my fault.

I note that my wife is at serious risk of falling in herself. She and the passer-by have both her arms now, and are beginning to pull, but the weight of the water on her clothes is dragging her down.

This is a genuine example of the butterfly-effect phenomenon, I muse to myself. Had our neighbour not had a party, this woman would not now be in the canal. It's a bit like in that movie *Sliding Doors*.

Finally, they pull the cyclist out. She sits, distressed, on the bank, soaking and breathless.

'Are you OK?' I ask her.

Saturday, 4 December 2004

I'm sitting in my office when an overpowering smell of burnt food fills the room. That's funny, I think.

I look out of the window. And then I notice it. My neighbour has had an extractor fan fitted, and the smells are getting trapped in the airlock between our houses and dispensing directly into my window.

'That's it!' I say out loud.

I march next door. I hear party noises. He opens the door.

'We have a problem,' I announce.

'I'm having a dinner party,' he says. 'I've burnt the dinner. This is a bad time.'

'I *know* you've burnt the dinner,' I say. 'Come.'

I lead him next door and make him sniff the air.

'Will you please move it?' I say.

'I'll think about it,' he says. 'Listen, now really isn't a good time . . .'

He goes back to his dinner party.

I am stunned. The words whirl around my head. 'I'll think about it . . .'

In my head, something happens. In my head he's still standing there.

'You'll *think* about it?' I say in my head.

'Yeah,' he drawls, in my head. 'I'll let you know my decision when I see fit.'

'Well, perhaps you'd like to think about *this*!' I yell in my head, waving Joel's wooden samurai sword replica at him, a wild look in my eyes. Then, in my head, the police arrive and arrest me. Then I'm in a cell, yelling through the slit, 'I didn't start it.'

And in real life I almost burst into tears at the injustice

of it all. So I find a bottle of whisky and take it next door and tell him that I don't want to fight with him.

'That's lovely of you,' he says, looking confused. 'I'll call my builders tomorrow to get this extractor fan moved.'

31 December 2004

We sit by the fire and talk about our New Year resolutions. Elaine says her hope for 2005 is that I'll start offering Joel moral guidance instead of giving into everything he asks for. I reply that my personal hope for 2005 is that she stops being stringent and snappy.

'I feel ready to watch *Enter the Dragon* now,' says Joel.

The DVD has been sitting there since Christmas Day like a Pandora's Box with the lid still on. My osteopath, a black belt in jeet kune do, had told me *Enter the Dragon* was suitable for six-year-olds.

'I think,' I say, for the fifth time this week, 'I have made an enormous mistake buying you *Enter the Dragon*.'

'Oh, let him watch it,' says Elaine. She wants to teach me a salutary lesson: Joel will be disturbed and it will be my fault.

And so we watch many necks being snapped followed by the scene where Bruce Lee's friend, Williams, has sex with four prostitutes.

'I'll take you, darling, and you and you and you,' drawls Williams. 'Please understand if I missed anyone, it's been a big day. I'm a little tired!'

Joel looks confused.

'Well, he's going to be doing a lot of cuddling tonight,' I quickly interject.

'Lucky guy!' says Joel.

'He's not at all disturbed!' I mouth, triumphantly, to Elaine.

Saturday, 8 January 2005

It is the summer of 1999. We are driving to the beach. We reach the Whitstable turning. I indicate left. 'Keep going!' yells Elaine.

'But the sign says Whitstable!' I yell.

'It's wrong!' she yells. 'The road system has changed since they put up the sign! *Keep going!*' I swerve in panic from lane to lane. Then I keep going.

'Hang on,' says Elaine, consulting the map. 'That was the right turning.'

'I *know*,' I yell.

'Then why did you keep going?' Elaine asks, incredulously.

'Because you told me to,' I say.

'Are you that weak?' asks Elaine.

I'll never forget this, I think. Never.

It is five and a half years later. I awake in a carefree mood. I jump out of the bed, poke my head through the closed curtains, and report on the weather to Elaine, who is still in bed.

'It's looking sunny but a little breezy today,' I say.

'*Will you just open the curtains and let me see for myself*,' Elaine unexpectedly yells.

'What?' I say, startled.

'The generous thing to do would be to fling the curtains open,' she says, 'but you bask in having information that I don't have access to. You do it every morning.'

'No I don't,' I say.

'Every morning,' she says. Then she mimics the kindly twinkle in my voice, the twinkle I had always assumed was charming: ' "It's a little cloudy." Or: "Oh dear, I hate to tell you this, Elaine, but it's raining." Just *open the curtains*!'

Elaine says this habit of mine has been making her quietly furious for ten years.

'Well maybe it is the *only moment* during the day that

I feel I have some *control*!' I yell. 'For instance, Whitstable? The turn-off? Remember?'

'What are you talking about?' says Elaine.

Saturday, 12 February 2005

We've been waiting forty-five minutes for our lunch. We
beckon the waiter.

'I'll check with the kitchen,' he says.

As he leaves, Elaine raises her eyebrows to say, 'This
restaurant is so inept.'

I shuffle in my chair.

'What?' says Elaine.

'Nothing,' I say.

'Go on,' she says.

'OK,' I say. 'You didn't check whether he was still
looking before you raised your eyebrows.'

'What?'

'You never do,' I say.

'Are you calling me rude?' says Elaine.

'It isn't a matter of rudeness,' I say. 'Everyone raises
their eyebrows to insult people behind their backs. I've
no problem with that. The thing is, you aren't *thorough*.
I'm so thorough I scan the room, even looking for things

like mirrors, to ensure there's absolutely no chance the person I'm raising my eyebrows about will notice. Whereas you do it the minute someone's out of *your* eye line. But how do you know he wasn't still looking?'

'*Was* he still looking?' asks Elaine.

'I don't know,' I say.

'Then why didn't you look,' says Elaine, 'if you care so much?'

'It isn't *my* responsibility,' I say. 'What? You want some kind of arrangement so that you insult, and then I instantly check? That sounds like a pretty complex ballet to me.'

'Maybe a restaurant would benefit from knowing their customers are unhappy,' says Elaine.

'But never in the form of a botched surreptitious raise of the eyebrows,' I say.

'So you'd rather furtively insult?' says Elaine.

'Yes!' I say.

'Coward.'

'No,' I say. 'I'm happy to confront, but if I follow even *that* up with the eyebrow-raise, I still ensure they aren't looking. You don't appreciate the power of the raised eyebrow, noticed in the peripheral vision of the person being insulted.'

'Whatever,' says Elaine.

Our food comes.

'That's brilliant,' I say to the waiter. 'Thank you so much.'

Tuesday, 1 March 2005

The Cardiff High School reunion is set for July. It's been twenty years! It'll take place in the pub near where we used to sneak off for cigarettes. The boys who threw me into Roath Park Lake will be in attendance.

The organizer emails me to ask if I can donate something for the raffle. I wonder if I should put together a package including my bestselling book, a photograph of me with my arm around Zoë Ball and a note saying, 'Sorry I missed you. Hopefully see you soon. Best, Nick Hornby.' I can call it *My Fantastic Life*.

Sunday, 20 March 2005

I phone my mother to wish her a happy Mother's Day.

'I'm amazed!' she says. 'This must be the first time you've ever phoned to wish me a happy Mother's Day.'

'Ha ha,' I say. 'So anyway, how are you?'

'Flabbergasted!' she says.

'Ha ha,' I say. 'So anyway, what's the news?'

'The news is that you've phoned to wish me a happy Mother's Day and I am absolutely gobsmacked,' she says.

'Ha ha,' I say. 'So what have you been up to?'

'Well, this morning I said to your father, "I bet Jonathan isn't going to phone to wish me a happy Mother's Day," and he said, "I bet he's not either." But you have! And I just can't believe it!'

'So other than you not believing that I'd phone, and then I did phone, and you were amazed,' I say, 'what's the news?'

'Hang on a second,' she says. '*David!*' she yells at my father. 'You're not going to believe who's on the phone and why! Jonathan! He's phoned to wish me a happy Mother's Day! I know! Incredible!'

I drum my fingers on the table. She comes back to the phone.

'Just amazing,' she says.

'So will you be doing anything special?' I ask, choosing my words carefully.

'Nothing could be as special, or at least as unique, as you calling to wish me a happy Mother's Day,' she says. 'Whatever we do for the rest of the day, I can tell you that it won't be as special as that.'

'And what will that be?' I ask.

'Probably discussing with your father how amazing it is that you called,' she says.

'Over dinner out?' I ask.

'On the way to dinner,' she says, 'during dinner, after dinner.'

'Anyway,' I say. 'Happy Mother's Day.'

'Thank you,' she says.

Monday, 21 March 2005

My father telephones to say he's restructuring his will again.

'You need to go to the Hong Kong and Shanghai Bank and find a manager and give him the following reference . . .' says my father.

'Where the hell is that?' I ask.

'Look it up!' says my father, exasperated.

I sigh and hang up. Only my father, with his financial-restructuring mania, would choose such a bizarre and esoteric bank. I type 'Bank of Shanghai HQ' into Google, mutter crossly and phone my father back.

'Their headquarters are in China!' I say.

'They'll have London branches,' he says.

'I've never seen one,' I snap, crossly.

'You surprise me,' he snaps back.

'Well, there's probably a branch somewhere in West London near the embassies,' I snap. 'So it's a trip to West London for me, then.'

'They have branches all over Cardiff,' he snaps.

'Well, I can only assume that Cardiff docks were a stopover for the tea trade between Shanghai and America and the branches grew up as a result of that, or something,' I snap.

'Maybe so,' snaps my father.

'Tell me the name again,' I snap.

'Hong Kong and Shanghai Banking Corporation,' he snaps.

There is a silence.

'HSBC?' I ask.

'Yes,' sighs my father.

For me the enduring mystery of this exchange is this: is my father the only person in Britain who refers to the HSBC by its full title, or am I the only person in Britain who didn't, until now, know what the acronym stands for?

Thursday, 14 April 2005

I inadvertently type my name into Google and accidentally press search. I discover that the *Western Mail*,

Wales's daily morning newspaper, has become interested in the fact that I was thrown into Roath Park Lake by some of my classmates. The newspaper has written: 'Did you take part in Jon Ronson's dunking? If so, give us a call on the news desk.'

I call the hotline to ask if anyone has phoned in yet.

'No,' says the journalist, David Williamson.

David assures me that if anyone gets in touch he will encourage them to express remorse.

'That's very kind of you,' I reply, touched.

Friday, 15 April 2005

I am considering wireless-connecting my home, although I don't know exactly what it means. A friend has done it and his North London house is now like NASA, full of bleeps and upstairs computers knowing what downstairs computers are doing. I dip my toe in the water by placing my mobile phone next to the bath. It rings. I lean over and pick it up.

'Hello?' I say.

It is a work colleague. We need to talk about contracts.

'Without a turnaround clause I'd be crazy to sign,' I

say. On the word crazy I gesture importantly with my hand and inadvertently instigate a small splashing sound.

There is a silence.

'Are you in the bath?' he asks.

'No,' I say.

I instantly lie as motionless as I possibly can.

'Really?' he says. 'It sounds like you're in the bath.'

I curse the fact that I randomly chose bath salts instead of bubble bath. The foam would have insulated the splashing noise. Is it too late? Can I pour bubble bath in and wave my hand around under the surface, thereby silently creating bubbles?

'I'm not in the bath,' I say.

'Oh,' he says, unsurely.

We continue the conversation, but it never quite recovers from this awkwardness. Our contract negotiations prove to be protracted. The water gets cold. My teeth chatter.

Tuesday, 31 May 2005

I am on holiday in Sardinia. A fellow Brit, who we met on the beach, comes to join us at our table. He seems perfectly nice, but who's to know?

'What are you watching on TV at the moment,' I shout over the band, playing 'Your Song'.

'*Shameless*,' he shouts.

'Do you like *Seinfeld*?' I shout.

'No,' he shouts. 'I hate it.'

He likes *Shameless* but hates *Seinfeld*? I think. Hmm.

'I like *Frasier*,' he shouts.

Frasier but not *Seinfeld*? I think. Strange.

I still can't work him out.

'Give yourselves a big cheer,' shouts the MC once 'Your Song' is over. 'You're all very special to have worked so hard to be able to stay in a place like this!'

The MC works the tables.

'Where are you from?'

'London,' I shriek into the microphone, thrilled to have been asked.

He approaches an expensively dressed, inscrutable middle-aged gentleman with an angry-looking wife.

'And you, sir?'

There is a silence.

'Moscow,' he finally replies, in a low growl.

'You're very welcome,' says the MC, backing off.

'What do you do?' asks the British man who has joined me at my table.

'I'm a writer,' I say.

The band starts playing another song.

'What sort of thing?' he shouts. I tell him. He nods.

'You mean a bit like Louis Theroux?' he shouts. 'I like him a lot.'

'He got it from me,' I shout.

I change the subject. I tell him about my impending school reunion.

'The truth is,' I shout, 'I'm dreading the reunion. It'll be a time of reckoning, a benchmark to judge our lives. Who is a failure? Who is disappointed?'

I suddenly feel incredibly miserable.

'Yes,' I shout, ruefully. 'The reunion will surely be bad for everyone.'

'Or maybe,' he shouts, 'you'll all get pissed and have a laugh.'

Thursday, 7 July 2005

It is the afternoon of the terrorist attacks and I find myself walking around London getting quietly annoyed with people who I feel aren't being stoical enough. I see a sign in a coffee shop on Upper Street that reads, 'Due to the events of today we will be closed until further notice.'

Until further notice? I think. That isn't very stoical.

Then I get a call from a friend, Simon, who sounds very shaken up.

'I missed the King's Cross explosion by about two minutes,' he explains. 'And then I travelled to Edgware Road and I must have missed that explosion by about three minutes. And I might actually have been killed if I hadn't stopped to talk to someone on the way to the Tube who delayed my journey by a few minutes. Anyway I'm upset and I'm going home early.'

That isn't very stoical, I think.

Friday, 8 July 2005

Simon calls me from work.

'How many times were you nearly killed on the way to work today?' I say.

'*It isn't funny*,' he shouts.

Saturday, 9 July 2005

Simon was right. It wasn't funny. It was just horrible.

Sunday, 10 July 2005

Today, the Queen praises London's 'resilience, sense of humour and courage'.

Yes, I think. That's all I was doing with Simon.

I was displaying the characteristics that make Britain great.

Monday, 11 July 2005

Simon telephones me from work.

'Don't worry, I wasn't almost killed on the way to work today!' he says. He sounds sheepish, as if he'd thought about my asinine remark and had come to the conclusion that he was indeed being over-dramatic, and his feelings of shock about being close to the explosions were not, after all, something he could talk about with friends.

Saturday, 16 July 2005

After much anxiousness about the school reunion, about meeting the boys who threw me in the lake twenty-two years ago, tonight it occurs. What I don't remember, it turns out, are the good times: the parties, listening to David Bowie, etc.

'Really?' I keep saying. 'We did that?'

'It's bizarre you don't remember that,' people keep replying. It's as if I've scrubbed from my memory anything that contradicts my image of school as the worst days of my life. Everyone is lovely all night. Then one of the chief lake-throwers approaches.

'I'm really upset about what you've been writing,' says Andy. (I'll call him Andy.) He insists I wasn't thrown in the lake. In fact, he says, we all jumped in together, in a frenzy of shared joy. Then we apparently all went back to his house to shower.

'You're fantasizing,' he says. 'You've got it all skewed. You think you were the only person in the lake?'

'I thought . . .' I say, unsurely.

'There are no bullies here,' he says. 'Just people who love you.'

We hug. Andy says that – with the exception of his children being born – Cardiff High was the happiest time of his life.

Just as I'm about to leave, a man called Paul comes over.

'I threw you in the lake,' he says. 'I did it because you were an arse. Andy helped. You were desperate to be popular, and so you got on everyone's tits. You seem exactly the same now, only not pubescent. Anyway, I'm not here to be judged.'

Paul walks away, turns back, and says, 'I think Andy's memory is clouded.'

Sunday, 24 July 2005

On Sunday mornings the Goths come to Starbucks. There are perhaps fifty of them. Many have upside-down crosses painted on their foreheads. Most wear rubber and latex, so I suppose they are Goth Fetishists. I wonder where they've been all night. Probably at a Goth Fetish club. I have to time my arrival impeccably to avoid being at the back of a long Goth queue. Today, I time it shoddily (8.05 a.m.), and I find myself midway. There's an old lady in the queue too. She looks terrified. I smile comfortingly at her to say, 'Don't fear the Goths. They are a gentle and basically middle-class subculture.'

This has been going on every Sunday morning for years now. I have frequently smiled comfortingly at old ladies in this manner. I am an unbiased third party who has chosen to tacitly reflect conviviality and warmth for the Goths. Apparently – a Starbucks barista once told me – the Goths have been banned from every coffee shop in the area, not because they've misbehaved but because the owners have felt prejudicial towards their aesthetics. This Starbucks is their last-chance saloon and I feel that my quietly compassionate stand has aided this equanimity.

Suddenly, two Goths jump the queue. They were behind me. Now they are in front. They've just jumped the queue! I am frozen with rage. After all I've done for them. I stand there for a moment, apoplectic, and then I march to the front.

'I think I ought to be served now,' I whisper, through gritted teeth, to the woman behind the counter. 'Two Goths jumped the queue. It's really rude.'

'I didn't see it happen,' she replies, flustered.

'They're just so *rude*,' I say.

'Just say something to them,' she whispers. 'Don't be scared. They won't hurt you.'

Tuesday, 26 July 2005

My trousers are fraying around the knees. They don't make them any more. I'll never find another pair like them. I have an idea.

Why the hell not? I think. I've earned it!

I make an appointment with a Savile Row tailor.

'Can you make an exact copy?' I ask.

They fuss around me. They say how beautifully my trousers hang from my legs. I notice the implication – that this is a reflection not only on the quality of my trousers but also on the quality of my legs.

They're just buttering me up, I think.

'Come and look at these beautiful trousers!' one tailor calls to another.

'Beautiful,' he replies, scrutinizing me as I stand in the middle of the room.

Why am I always putting myself down? I think. Maybe my legs *do* wear trousers well.

'I'm going to outsource them to a wonderful tailor,' says Emily, who runs the business. 'He's really a maestro. He's among the very best tailors in London. He's fabulous.'

'Wonderful!' I say.

'Fabulous and kind of . . .' She pauses. 'Difficult,' she adds, brightly. 'Like a fabulous, brilliant perfectionist.'

'Kind of brilliant but troubled?' I ask.

'Exactly,' she says.

'That *does* sound good,' I say.

Emily calls the next day. 'Great news,' she says. 'He'll have them ready in a week!'

'Wonderful!' I say.

Monday, 1 August 2005

I call Emily.

'I spoke to him just this morning,' she says. 'He says he simply won't hand them over until he's absolutely satisfied with them. He says just wait one more week. It'll be worth it!'

'Wonderful!' I say. 'Thank you so much!'

Friday, 26 August 2005

I call Emily about the trousers. There is no news. She says she's as annoyed about it as I am.

'I went into Gap yesterday,' I say. I allow a silence to linger menacingly in the air. Then I add, 'When I was there I tried on a pair of trousers.'

'Don't do that,' she says.

'I'm almost at the stage where I have no choice,' I say. (This is a lie: I have three or four perfectly good pairs of trousers left.)

'I'll chase him up again right away,' says Emily.

I put the phone down and I write 'Chase Up Tailor' in my diary for Friday. Then I turn to the following Friday and I write: 'Chase Up Tailor'.

Monday, 5 September 2005

Emily calls to say the tailor has gone AWOL.

'Well, that's just great,' I say.

Wherever he is, she adds, he's taken my almost finished trousers with him.

Tuesday, 6 September 2005

Emily calls. Her voice sounds small.

'He's had a stroke,' she says.

There is a silence.

'He should never have taken the job on,' she says. 'He's an idiot. Like so many tailors, he's paranoid that work will dry up. So he takes on everything. He can't say no. And I'm phoning him every five minutes, "Where are the trousers? Where are the trousers?"'

I cough. 'Could it have been my trousers that . . .?' I ask.

'Don't go there, Jon,' says Emily.

'Is there anyone else who can finish them?' I ask.

Tuesday, 13 September 2005

We are on holiday in Italy, and I am fulfilling a long-held ambition. I've embarked upon a significant walk. I'm walking alone to Vernazza, along treacherous cliff-tops with no railings, a gruelling two-hour trek. I have water and cigarettes and my PalmPilot in a plastic carrier bag. My T-shirt is soaked in sweat, and I feel alive.

As I walk, I think about North Korea. Before I set off, Elaine and I watched a CNN report in which Kim Jong-Il's officials spoke of how the inherently wicked Americans were obsessively, and enviously, conspiring to destroy them.

'I'll never understand,' said Elaine as we watched, 'how some people can allow their minds to spiral so irrationally.'

'Mystifying,' I agreed. 'Paranoid.'

'Nuts,' she said.

Ahead of me, along this perilous cliff path, I hear American voices. There's a group of them. They look ex-military, in their late fifties, big and muscular, some with handlebar moustaches, relaxing in a shady glen. One is blocking my way, his back to me.

'Excuse me,' I cough. He turns around.

'You wanna get past?' he growls. 'You need to pay a toll!'

'I am paying,' I say. 'In sweat!'

They laugh heartily.

'You can say *that* again!' he says.

'My Special Forces training down at Fort Bragg has certainly stood me in good stead for this walk!' I say.

They laugh a lot.

This banter is going extremely well, I think, pleased with myself.

'You ever see combat?' he asks.

'Nam!' I say. They laugh uproariously.

I'm doing brilliantly, I think.

'You got anything to sell?' he asks, glancing at my plastic bag.

'I got *shawls*!' I say.

'What?' he says.

'Lovely shawls!' I say. 'You want? Cheap price!'

The Americans descend into a baffled silence. I don't get it. The shawl banter is, to my mind, just as funny as the Nam banter. He turns to his friend.

'What's he saying?' he asks, loudly.

'Dunno. Something about shawls,' his friend replies.

'*Have you got anything to sell me in that plastic bag?*' he asks me again, slowly.

111

Suddenly, it dawns on me. This isn't an invitation for me to continue bantering. It is a coded request for drugs. They think I'm a dope-dealer.

'No, I haven't,' I say, sounding hurt.

I storm off down the path.

'Americans!' I inwardly mutter. 'Subjugating me.'

I get back to the hotel in time for my pre-arranged late breakfast with Elaine. She is standing, glowering, at the self-service All-Bran dispenser.

'What?' I say.

'They're rationing the cereal,' she says. 'I put a little cereal into my bowl and now the dispenser won't give me any more.'

I examine the dispenser. It is true.

'I think it's terrible,' says Elaine, 'the amount we're paying, that you only get a tiny bit of All-Bran.'

'It's exploitative,' I agree.

I stand there, shooting paranoid glares at the waiters, the dispenser.

Then a waiter approaches, and says, 'Oh. I think it's stuck again.'

He gives the dispenser a shake. All-Bran falls out into Elaine's bowl.

'Oh,' says Elaine.

The madness should end there, but sadly it does not.

'Look at *that*!' says Elaine, gesturing at the breakfast menu. 'This is supposed to be B *and* B,' she says. 'But the menu says we need to pay for everything other than coffee and pastries. *Even orange juice.* Look: one euro for orange juice. Three euros for fruit salad.'

'But it's a self-service buffet,' I say. 'There's no way they'd be able to ascertain what we ate. What? You think they're going to examine the debris of our breakfast table after we leave and look for crumbs and bits of fruit and calculate what we ate beyond pastries? This is you all over. You get these thoughts in your head and they spiral!'

I knock my head with my forefinger and make a spirally motion.

'Look at that!' says Elaine, staring in the direction of a nearby waiter who is scrutinizing a recently vacated breakfast table.

'He's not *investigating the debris*,' I say. 'He's . . .'

'What?'

'*I don't know . . . preparing himself to tidy up!*' I say in a snarled whisper.

'When have you ever seen a waiter *prepare* to tidy up?' Elaine counters. 'They just tidy up.'

A waiter approaches.

'Is everything OK?' he asks.

'Fine,' smile Elaine and I in unison.

As he leaves, Elaine raises her eyebrows as if to say, 'What an inept hotel.'

'You're doing it again,' I snarl.

'What?' snarls Elaine.

'You didn't check whether he was still looking before you raised your eyebrows. You did it the minute he was out of *your* eye line. You have no *concept* of whether or not he was still looking.'

'*Was* he still looking?' asks Elaine.

'*I* don't know,' I say.

I glance over at the recently vacated nearby table. The waiter is only just beginning to tidy up the plates.

'He did seem to be scrutinizing the plates for an awfully long time,' I admit.

'See?' says Elaine.

'Well,' I say. 'There's no way I'm going to *help* them sting us for fruit salad.'

I grab the bowl and start scraping the final remnants clean with my napkin.

'I'm putting my feelings about this in the hotel guest survey questionnaire,' Elaine mutters as I scrape.

'Like they *care*!' I say.

A waiter approaches. 'Is there anything else I can get you?' he asks.

'Just the bill,' I say sullenly.

'Oh no, it's all included in your room rate,' he says. We go to the beach.

Thursday, 10 November 2005

An American movie star has moved into our street. I sometimes catch her eye through the window as she walks past the house. When this happens, my body involuntarily thrusts itself backwards behind the curtains, as if propelled by the sheer force of her celebrity. This morning she saw me and gave me a wave, and I waved back and mouthed 'Hi!' whilst simultaneously lurching out of sight. I suspect she's beginning to see me as a curtain-twitcher, but nothing could be further from the truth.

I fear this is going to be a Peter Straus scenario all over again. A few years ago I got myself into a vicious spiral of inelegance whenever I was in proximity to the publisher and agent Peter Straus. There was no explanation for it – Peter Straus is no more intimidating than anyone else – but it became a self-fulfilling prophecy, and it culminated in an incident at a literary party at the Wallace Collection in central London.

The party took place in a lavish marble conservatory around a lovely fountain. I walked in, saw Peter Straus, and thought, Why is it that whenever Peter Straus is around I do something stupid? I am going to break the curse, wander over to him and have a nice chat. Here I go.

I moved forward, gave him a casual wave and immediately fell into the fountain. I emerged to see hundreds of novelists staring at me.

Now the movie star on our street has seen me dart behind my curtain three times. This is how it begins. I must break the curse.

There is a knock on the door. It is her. She says she just wanted to say hello and introduce herself.

'*Elaine!*' I shout. 'We have a visitor!'

We sit in the kitchen.

'I see you have dogs,' says Elaine. 'We see you *walking* your dogs. You should take your dogs to the celebrity dog-pampering centre in Primrose Hill. Lots of celebrities take their dogs there.'

'Thanks,' she says.

I wince. Elaine never talks like this. She seems to be presenting herself in a wholly alien manner.

'I tell you what I am looking for,' she says. 'A good local hairdresser.'

'There's a wonderful one down in Bloomsbury . . .' Elaine begins.

Don't say it, I think.

'Lots of celebrities get their hair cut there,' says Elaine.

I cough. 'Tell me,' I say. I pause. 'When you are making a movie and you have to wait for ages to film a scene, *what do you do to pass the time?*' This last line comes out as a screech.

'Backgammon,' she says.

After she leaves, Elaine and I glance at each other, exhausted.

'You mentioned the word celebrity too often,' I say.

'It was the elephant in the room,' she says.

'The phrase "elephant in the room",' I say, 'means the thing that everyone is aware of but leaves unsaid. Her celebrity was not, by that criterion, the elephant in the room.'

We fall into a rueful silence.

'We've done it again, haven't we?' says Elaine.

Tuesday, 15 November 2005

In general, if a Sunday broadsheet newspaper announces that an impending disaster (a meteorite, anthrax, whatever) is about to destroy the world, I don't believe it. Oh, silly Sunday broadsheet journalists, I think, always getting into a flap about the end of the world!

But if a Monday newspaper says the same thing, I do.

'Are you worried about bird flu?' asks a friend, Caitlin. She's here for Sunday lunch with her husband and two small children.

'No,' I say, mysteriously.

'Why not?' she asks.

'Because,' I say, and I notice my voice is sounding unexpectedly creepy, 'I've got Tamiflu.'

There's a silence. I notice Caitlin glancing at her two small children, running happily around the kitchen.

'How did you get it?' she asks, feigning non-jealousy.

'From the Internet.' I smile.

She relaxes and grins. 'It's probably fake,' she says.

'Oh, it's genuine,' I say.

'It might *not* be genuine,' she says.

'It's genuine,' I say, testily. 'I checked with Roche. I emailed Roche the serial numbers, and details of the online pharmacy, and a description of what the box looked like, and Roche emailed me back and said it was genuine. Look!'

I get the packets out of the medicine cabinet.

Actually, I don't believe that an avian-flu pandemic will hit. I base this assessment on the fact that we didn't all die of CJD, and also I have an idea that the sort of people who don't believe in the imminence of a bird-flu pandemic are enlightened freethinkers and that's how I like to see myself.

Nonetheless, I put them away again and close the door a little too quickly. I make a weird mental note to myself to move the Tamiflu somewhere else in the house when the pandemic hits just in case Caitlin and her family are stricken with the virus and, in a desperate last-ditch attempt to save their own lives, break in with brickbats, or whatever, and steal our Tamiflu. They are lovely people from Crouch End, Caitlin and her family, but even the lovely will stop at nothing to save themselves when a pandemic hits, I ponder ruefully. Maybe I could have a series of cubbyholes and rotate the Tamiflu's location, a little like they do with Dick Cheney.

'I need to get Tamiflu,' says Caitlin.

Well, good luck! I think. 'I got mine a few months ago *before* the panic buying,' I explain. 'You should be careful because now, of course, there *is* a lot of fake Tamiflu around. Roche told me that in their email.'

'Well, anyway,' she says, relaxing again, 'apparently the H5N1 strain is becoming resistant to Tamiflu.'

'*One* Vietnamese girl,' I correct her, 'was found to be resistant.'

Why, I think, is she so eager to diss my Tamiflu? Is she thinking, deep down, Yes, our lack of foresight might have sealed our death sentences but at least we can go to our graves safe in the knowledge that the Ronsons will die too?

'Do you want to go halves on a ventilator?' she asks suddenly.

'Whose house would the ventilator be stored in?' I ask.

'Those are the kinds of details that could be worked out later,' she says.

There's a silence. I narrow my eyes.

'I think we'll be OK with the Tamiflu,' I say.

Monday, 28 November 2005

I'm in an osteopath's waiting room, thinking about a terrible moment that occurred a few weeks ago, when a mutual friend invited me to have dinner with the American comedian Jon Stewart, who was over in London with his writers and producer. The dinner was going very well and so I relaxed. I relaxed too much, I think, because I announced to the table how much I was enjoying *Space Cadets*.

'What's *Space Cadets*?' asked Jon Stewart's producer.

'It's this *really funny conceit*,' I said. 'They get ten *really stupid* contestants and tell them that they're blasting them into space, but they're *not*! It's a hoax! It's all faked in a shuttle that was a prop from the movie *Armageddon*, or something.'

The table fell silent.

'I have a problem with that,' said one of Jon Stewart's writers. 'It sounds horrible and exploitative.'

I froze. I too believe *Space Cadets* to be horrible, so why was I now enthusing about it to the table?

'It *is* horrible,' I said, lamely. 'But it's funny to watch.'

'I'm sure it is,' said someone from Jon Stewart's party. 'But that's not the point, is it?'

I changed the subject. I said how coincidental it was that all the big children's movies this Christmas included scenes of animals dying – penguins, Aslan and King Kong – and the moment passed. The rest of the dinner was fine, and I doubt they even remembered the *Space Cadets* incident by the end. But now, in the osteopath's waiting room, the scene replays itself in my mind. I cringe.

'Jon Ronson?' calls the osteopath.

I follow him into his office. I've never visited this osteopath before, and so I do what I always do with new osteopaths: I try and get him to slag off all my previous osteopaths. In the mutual slagging off of my previous osteopaths, I find concord and comfort with new osteopaths.

'And then,' I say, 'in over-massaging the pinched nerve, he must have irritated the nerve next to it, because on the Saturday my left arm literally felt like it was being dipped in boiling oil.'

'I can't comment on that,' says Frank.

I glance at him. What's up with Frank? I think. I try again.

'It is clear he irritated my median nerve,' I say.

'I'm sorry,' says Frank, 'but I am an osteopath, and so I just won't be critical of other osteopaths.'

Huh? I think. One thing that usually unites osteopaths is their willingness to bad-mouth other osteopaths.

'Now can you lie on the bed?' he says.

I do.

Saturday, 10 December 2005

We are walking down the street when we pass a newspaper billboard that reads 'HUNT FOR KILLER SANTA INTENSIFIES'.

Joel stops and reads it.

'What's going on?' he asks.

'Actually,' I say, 'the headline is referring to the fact that Santa murdered someone.'

'What are you talking about?' Joel asks.

'Yes,' I say. 'Santa murdered someone, which certainly brings a whole new meaning to the words, "You'd better watch out, you'd better not cry, you'd better not shout!"'

That has to be one of the funniest jokes I've ever thought of, I think, thrilled with myself.

'I don't understand what you're talking about,' says Joel. 'Why did Santa kill someone?'

But I am oblivious to these questions.

'I'll tell you something else that's just plain wrong about Santa being a murderer,' I add, on a tremendous roll. 'That kind of behaviour is a bit rum coming from a man whose job description includes making an annual moral assessment on whether *we've* been naughty or nice!'

I laugh a lot.

'What are you talking about?' Joel asks. 'I really don't understand. Will you just explain?'

'Talk about the pot calling the kettle black!' I say. 'There he is, suggesting we'd better be good for goodness' sake or we won't get any presents, and all the while he's *murdering people*!'

Then I go quiet and start to improvise to myself: 'Making a list . . . um . . . sleigh bells . . . um . . . sees you when you're sleeping . . .'

'Will you just shut up,' hisses Elaine.

'What?' I say, lost in my thoughts, trying to decide whether I've exhausted the gag or whether it's worth coming up with something about Santa murdering you in your sleep.

'He's only *seven*,' hisses Elaine.

I look at Joel. He seems fine.

'Oh, come on,' I say. 'Joel knows the real Santa didn't murder anyone. It was someone *dressed* as Santa.'

'How did he murder him?' asks Joel.

'Can we just keep walking?' says Elaine.

'I think it was a stabbing,' I say. 'Or a bludgeoning.'

'What's a bludgeoning?' asks Joel.

Elaine shakes her head sadly.

'It's nothing that he hasn't seen time and again on *Power Rangers*,' I say.

'They never bludgeon people to death on *Power Rangers*,' Elaine says.

'They're *always* bludgeoning people on *Power Rangers*,' I say.

'If you tell me what bludgeoning is,' says Joel, 'I'll tell you if they do it on *Power Rangers*.'

'Smashing someone's head repeatedly until they die,' I say.

'Santa does that?' says Joel.

Tuesday, 13 December 2005

Occasionally, if I'm saying something funny to someone, I imagine that anyone who happens to overhear it is also finding it funny, and is stopping whatever they're doing to listen to me, rapt and grateful. I'm not like this normally, but something kicks in when I'm riding the crest of a funny remark. Everything goes giddy, and I lose all sense of perspective. It's like I've been injected with adrenaline.

Today I'm on the phone, telling my friend Stephen my joke about the man who recently committed a murder whilst dressed as Santa.

'And this is someone whose job description includes making an annual moral assessment on whether *we've* been naughty or nice!' I say.

Stephen laughs.

Elaine bursts in. 'The electrician needs your help,' she says.

An electrician is downstairs in the kitchen looking at our cooker hood.

'OK, OK, in a second,' I say. 'Honestly.'

I turn away from her. 'She'd go crazy if I interrupted *her* like that while *she* was on the phone,' I say to Stephen. It's true. Elaine didn't even give me a look to say 'Can I say something to you?' She just burst in and interrupted.

Then I think, I suppose the nice thing to do would be to finish the hilarious thing I'm saying to Stephen whilst walking downstairs to the kitchen.

So I do. I wander downstairs, the phone to my ear. I smile at the electrician, and say to Stephen, 'It certainly gives a whole new meaning to the words, "You'd better watch out, you'd better not cry, you'd better . . ."'

'Will you *get off the phone and help the electrician,*' says Elaine.

'In a *minute*!' I say. Then I add, tartly, 'The whole world doesn't stop just because *you* want it to!'

I shoot the electrician a conspiratorial grin. Then I turn on my heels, furrow my brow and think to myself, Both times I just glanced at the electrician, there was something strange going on, but what? Let me think. He didn't smile back and he looked to be in pain.

I glance at him again. His legs are buckling against the massive weight of the cooker hood, which he's desperately attempting to hold up, to stop it from crashing onto his head, and attached to the cooker hood is a three-storey-high silver air duct.

'Elaine didn't explain!' I shriek. 'I'm *so sorry*!'

I rush over and help shoulder the weight. 'She didn't explain!' I repeat, but the electrician says nothing. Not a single word. He just looks at me with pure, undisguised hatred.

I think about the electrician when I visit my new osteopath later. I cringe and flinch.

'Relax,' says the osteopath. 'You're very tense.'

And then he starts to tell me a very strange anecdote.

This is only the second time I've visited this osteopath. His surgery is in a basement flat near Wood Green, North London, which is a bit creepy. I don't know him. I found him randomly on the Internet. I'm visiting someone's basement flat that I discovered on the Internet, and I'm topless and he's rubbing my back. Thank God he's wearing a white coat, is all I can say. Thank God he has a model of a spinal cord on his desk, otherwise I would be freaked out.

'So anyway,' he says. 'A bunch of us went skiing and we started playing a game that one of us had invented. The game went like this. I wrote a name down on a piece of paper. Someone else wrote down an event. A third person wrote down the outcome of the event. Then we muddled up all the pieces of paper and . . .'

It's Consequences, I think. He's describing the game Consequences. Doesn't he realize this?

I cough and open my mouth to say, 'What you're describing is actually a well-known game called Consequences.'

But something stops me. I don't know this man. He made such a big deal of the fact that a member of his party invented the game, if I disabuse him of this, will he go crazy? Plus, why is he enthusiastically describing a game of Consequences to me anyway? I know one shouldn't over-analyse small talk, but this talk is unnervingly small. I try and change the subject.

'I think my last osteopath did permanent damage to my median nerve,' I say.

'And then we adapted the game,' he says, 'so the things we wrote down had to have fruit-related puns. Like, "Zestfully he went to . . ."'

It's *Consequences with fruit*, I think, alarmed. Can't he *see* that?

'You're very tense,' he says. 'Relax your muscles.' Then he says, 'You know, I'm not really an osteopath. Oh no, I just pretend to be an osteopath to get people to come to my flat!'

'Ha ha ha,' I say, thinking, I don't like being in an awkward situation with someone who tries to alleviate the awkwardness by making reference to it. What I prefer is being in an awkward situation with someone who feels equally awkward, and neither of us mentions it, and it goes away of its own accord. I wish he'd be more like that.

'I think I need to see you in a month,' he says. 'Shall we make an appointment?'

'OK,' I say.

Friday, 6 January 2006

I take Joel to see *Charlie and the Chocolate Factory*. When Veruca Salt appears I whisper, 'You know who she reminds me of?'

'Emma?' he says.

'Yes!' I say.

Emma is a little girl we know. We laugh.

'See how clever Roald Dahl is,' I say, 'spotting the universal ways that children behave. That's what writers do, you see? They work out what's known as "universal character traits". See?'

'Yes!' replies Joel.

I'm like a brilliant English teacher, I think, bringing English vividly to life. I am like one of those inspirational English teachers.

Tuesday, 10 January 2006

Joel has developed a phobia of Muslim women in burkas, believing they are actually Black Ninjas, the villains in the martial-arts movie that has been swirling around in his head ever since I let him watch *Enter the Dragon*. He thinks any minute they'll lunge at him and he must be constantly prepared. I'd like to introduce him to one, to prove they aren't Black Ninjas, but I don't know any. I can hardly approach one at random and say, 'I'm sorry, but could you explain to my son that you are a normal person like we are,' which is what Joel has been urging me to do.

The *Enter the Dragon* DVD is now in a cupboard out of his reach. Elaine put it there along with an Eminem DVD I brought him. It is the cupboard of presents that turned out to not be great ideas. Sometimes I don't think things through.

I'm out with Joel when a Muslim woman in a burka approaches.

'Excuse me,' she says. 'Do you know the way to Old Street?'

'*Yes!*' I say. 'You go down there, and then when you get to the bottom . . .'

I am so eager to have the chance to display my local knowledge that I am providing detailed instructions even though I am not entirely sure what I'm talking about. There is a possibility that I am directing her to the wrong place. It isn't cruelty. Cruelty is the last thing on my mind. It is more the inebriating, dizzying allure of being able to provide instant assistance to someone in need, combined with the faint realization that it doesn't matter if I send them to the wrong place because they can always ask someone else and I'll never see them again anyway. Perhaps the look of gratitude on the face of a stranger in response to a display of local knowledge is such a fantastically potent, short-term hit that I blind myself to the long-term consequences of my unwillingness to admit an inability to help.

I shoot Joel a glance that says, 'Don't you *dare* ask her if she's a Black Ninja.'

'And then turn left . . .' I say.

I'm being so kind, I think. Look at how I'm really pulling out the stops to help. I'm kind of building bridges between the Muslim and the Jewish communities here. I'm showing her that Jews are *good*. And I've managed to convey silently to Joel that it is *not* acceptable to ask her if she's a Black Ninja. I'm juggling a lot of complicated stuff here and I'm doing really well.

'Thank you,' she says, and leaves.

Wednesday, 11 January 2006

It is pouring with rain. Finally, after half an hour, I manage to flag down a taxi.

'Well, I'm certainly glad to see you!' I say, convivially. He says nothing.

That's funny, I think.

'Upper Street, please,' I say.

He motions with his head for me to get in. I am in an unusually gregarious mood. I turn on the intercom.

'Have you seen the advert on TV,' I say, 'that says a particular shampoo will make your hair "not once, but *twice* as shiny"?' I pause before delivering the zinger. 'But surely if, after washing your hair, it appears "once" as shiny, that equates to *exactly* as shiny as it was before you shampooed it. My point is, twice as shiny is not so great!'

There is a silence. Then, suddenly, incredibly, I see the red intercom light go dark. Without a word, he has switched me off.

I am crushed. It is rare that I am this enchanting in taxis. I want to tell him how unusually generous I am being with my wit. Then I feel scared. Surely only a deeply troubled man would respond in this eerie a manner to my shampoo-advert observation.

I get home shortly before Joel's friend Emma comes round.

The moment she arrives, Joel says to her. 'You're just like Veruca Salt!'

Emma looks crushed.

'My *dad* thinks you're just like Veruca Salt too!' he says.

'No, I don't,' I snarl. 'And who did I say *you* were like? Mike TV. I said Emma may be a tiny bit like Veruca Salt but you are *just* like Mike TV. You're *Mike TV*. Yes you *are*.'

'You never said I was like Mike TV,' says Joel.

Sunday, 15 January 2006

Tonight, Joel is spending the night at his friend's house. This will be his first ever sleepover: the first night in seven years that Elaine and I will be able to do whatever we like. I suggest we see the 6.15 p.m. showing of *Grizzly Man*, have dinner and be home by, say, 10.30 p.m. Elaine agrees.

'It sounds very nice,' she says.

This is a relief for me. I was concerned she might want to go to a nightclub. I've had a secret worry that when Joel leaves home, in eleven years' time, Elaine will want to become active, pulling me into all kinds of energetic pursuits, so I'm glad there's no harbinger of that today.

'*You* choose the restaurant!' I say, feeling bad about the many restrictions I've imposed on the evening.

She goes off, and starts researching restaurants on the

Internet. I don't understand why she's doing this. Why can't we just eat somewhere we already know about? Still, I don't say anything.

'We're going to Dans Le Noir!' she calls.

'OK!' I say.

She comes into the room.

'And let's get a rickshaw there!' she says.

There's a silence.

'It'll be fun!' she says. 'After the film, we'll jump into a rickshaw!'

I stare at Elaine. She has an excited grin on her face. I can see she means it. I don't want to hurt her feelings, so I don't yell, 'There's *no way* I'm getting into a rickshaw. What are you *becoming*?'

'OK!' I say. 'A rickshaw!'

Later, I look up Dans Le Noir on the Internet: 'A restaurant where guests dine in complete darkness, the idea being that losing one's sense of sight enhances one's sense of taste.'

Why the hell would I want to do *that*? I think.

Then I think, Actually, it sounds like fun.

Suddenly, I feel invigorated by Elaine's unexpected joie de vivre. Yes! I think. It'll be a completely new experience!

I close my eyes and imagine myself eating in the dark. Hah! I think. Wow.

Four hours later. Joel is at his friend's house. *Grizzly Man* is just finishing. During the film a thought kept popping into my head: 'I hope Elaine has forgotten about this whole rickshaw business.'

Whenever I've seen people in rickshaws, I've seen people trapped, exposed. Yes, they smile. But they look like anxious, dutiful smiles to me: the smiles of young, courting couples who don't want to hurt one another's feelings and are consequently *pretending* to enjoy their romantic rickshaw ride. Whereas Elaine and I have been married for *years*. Why should I be worried about hurting her feelings? Surely it's fine to hurt her feelings after a decade of marriage?

We leave the cinema.

Please don't say it, I think.

'Let's get that rickshaw!' she says.

I tell Elaine I'm not willing to get a rickshaw.

'You'd get a rickshaw if Joel wanted a rickshaw,' she says.

This is true. If Joel wanted a rickshaw ride I'd leap delightedly into a rickshaw. But I don't want to have a rickshaw ride with my wife. Why is this? Could it be that I've compartmentalized my domestic life so that everything fun I do, I do with Joel, and everything not fun I do, I do with Elaine? I find this too stressful to consider so I change the subject.

'I've got something *amazing* to tell you,' I say. 'When you see an empty plastic bottle on the ground, does it usually have its lid on or off?'

'Off,' says Elaine.

'Exactly,' I say. 'Who'd take the trouble to put a lid back onto a bottle they're about to discard? However, almost every time you see a discarded *Lucozade* bottle, it has its lid on! I swear to God! Only Lucozade!'

'How do you know?' asks Elaine, dubiously.

'The photographer Stephen Gill told me, and since then I've seen two discarded Lucozade bottles *both with their lids on*! I tell you,' I say, 'it's an observation worthy of Malcolm Gladwell. *Taxi!*' I call. The taxi pulls up. 'Dans Le Noir!' I say.

We arrive at the restaurant. It turns out that you order your food in a well-lit bar and then, when the dinner is ready, you put anything that lights up, like a phone or a lighter, into a locker. A blind waiter leads you into pitch-blackness, sits you down and you eat. I sense frostiness from Elaine because of the abandoned rickshaw idea, and so in the bar I am enthusiasm itself.

'Eating in the dark!' I say, shaking my head with excited disbelief. 'Wow!'

There's silence from Elaine. The Lucozade-bottle observation went down well earlier, so I try and alleviate the tension by making another observation.

'It is never a good idea to show sea-life in travel adverts,' I say. 'Who wants to swim amid sea-life?'

'What?' says Elaine.

'You don't want underwater camera shots of, you know, jellyfish and, um, fish, in TV adverts for beach holidays, is all I'm saying,' I say.

We've been here twenty minutes. '*Hello?*' I shout across the bar. 'Can someone give us a *menu?*'

An hour passes. Nobody takes our order. I'm hungry and tired. I glare accusingly at the sighted managers, barging around with clipboards. One barged too close to me as I went to the toilet, and I nearly fell over. As I practically toppled I ruefully thought: I'd have assumed that managers who make a special effort to provide job opportunities for blind people would be especially nice. But *oh no*.

Finally we order: the 'surprise'.

'Stop panicking,' mutters Elaine. 'It's just a night out.'

Our blind waiter Brian welcomes us. He leads us through a set of curtains into the pitch-blackness.

'Wow!' I say, making an effort. Brian sits us down.

'If you need anything, just call for me,' he says. And he leaves us alone.

'Elaine?' I say.

I know she's there. But she says nothing.

I resort to the one, admittedly extreme, tactic that

never fails to cheer us up: slagging off friends of ours who I believe aren't as good parents as us.

'I tell you who are really terrible parents,' I say, feeling around for my water. 'Bob and Ellen! They practically abuse their children through neglect. Don't you think?'

Expressing superiority over people we know is just the tonic this frosty moment needs, I think. But in the darkness, there is silence. I cough.

Elaine screams.

'*What?*' I yell, shocked.

'It's some kind of fish,' she screeches. '*Feel.*'

She grabs my wrist and drapes a piece of smoked fish over my hand.

'I don't like it here,' she says in a quivering voice.

That's *it*, I think. I've been making a very big effort to be nice, and this is costing £100. And all I'm hearing is negativity.

'Well, all I can say is I hope you never develop a serious disability because you'd be lousy at handling it!' I shout.

'*Ssshhh!*' says a Frenchman from somewhere. 'It is dangerous to talk too loudly in the dark.'

I sniff the fish. It smells horrible. 'My senses are being awakened, but in a bad way,' I say.

'Yes,' says Elaine, cheering up. Finally we're getting

on, united by attacking the concept of smelling smoked fish in the dark.

'I bet if they turned the lights on,' says Elaine, 'the place would be decorated terribly.'

I need to go to the toilet. 'Brian?' I call. 'Brian?'

Friday, 27 January 2006

When I began writing these columns, eighteen months ago, I received a telephone call from a Scottish film director who said he wanted to turn them into a movie. He had just returned from living in Los Angeles and he invited me to his home in the Cotswolds.

He said, 'I think we need something else, some kind of life-changing crisis. What if . . .' He paused. 'What if,' he said, 'the "you" is working abroad somewhere, away from your family, somewhere hot and glamorous, and you embark upon a stupid affair with a young girl. Someone half your age. So you embark upon a torrid but incredibly ill-advised affair with a beautiful young girl . . .'

'Like a kind of midlife-crisis type of affair?' I asked.

He looked slightly offended.

'I wouldn't necessarily say that,' he said. 'But certainly

a moment-of-madness type of affair. And it puts your entire family in jeopardy.'

I thought about this.

'Does the "wife" find out?' I asked.

'No,' he said. 'She never finds out.'

I nodded thoughtfully.

'OK!' I said.

The film business being what it is, however, the movie never came to pass. Now, however, I've been approached by another film company. They want to turn these columns into a movie.

'There's just one thing,' they say, when I meet them this week at their Central London offices. 'We kind of need something else. The "you" needs to have some kind of life-changing crisis. So how would you feel if the "wife" is, say . . .'

They pause and look at each other.

One of them coughs.

'Dead,' they say.

'OK!' I say.

Sunday, 29 January 2006

I've ended up on a strange cc list. A group of physicists working – sometimes up on high – within the CIA and

US military intelligence email each other, often thirty times a day, and one of them has mysteriously decided to copy the emails to me. Mostly they drone on about 'Q<>(X)' and so last week I wrote to say, 'Thank you for sending me all these emails, but I haven't got a clue what you're talking about, so you should probably stop.'

The physicist emailed back, 'It appears that Colin Bennett was right after all, and you are an idiot.'

I have no idea who Colin Bennett is, nor why he's telling a CIA physicist that I'm an idiot. I really don't know how I ended up on this list. But the emails are still coming, and I always scan them, just in case. How often does one get sent private conversations between physicists working within US intelligence?

Today, one of them emails the others to say he's had an awful idea. How about this, he writes: 'An Iranian terrorist takes a trip to neighbouring Turkey. He grabs a bird with bird flu. He sticks it in a room with a number of fellow terrorists who've infected themselves with ordinary flu. The virus mutates. The terrorists go to airports and they cough.

'The result,' he continues, 'might be millions and millions of dead infidels. Just a bunch of people flying around, breathing.'

Oh my God, I think with mounting horror. That could happen.

I form a nightmarish mental picture of cruel-eyed fluey terrorists angrily ordering one another to get closer to the chicken. Then I think, Hang on – surely all this is asking a virus to do an awful lot?

The physicists start emailing each other furiously. One suggests that's nothing. Who cares about bird flu when 'the US will launch a nuclear attack on Iran within three months. You have less than three months to decide what to do with your life.'

So what, another ruefully reasons – America is, for all intent and purpose, dead anyway: 'Kids go home from school and, rather than do their homework, they watch MTV, have group sex and get high. [Take] the appearance of the new high school super slut, who makes a decision to copulate with at least 100 guys before she graduates.'

Are these physicists sharing their nightmare fantasies with their CIA employers? Could all this be having an impact on the war on terror?

I consider myself an unusually neurotic person. I once convinced myself that my son had Premature Ageing syndrome because a few people told me he looked old for his age. I am, I now realize, far, far less paranoid than a bunch of scientists working high up within the CIA. This is not good.

Monday, 30 January 2006

I walk to Starbucks, stopping for cigarettes along the way. The health warning reads, 'Smoking causes ageing of the skin'.

Well, I don't mind that!

I listen to my pocket DAB personal radio as I walk. There's a report on about throat cancer, so I do what I always do when stories about cancer of the lung or throat come on the radio: I switch channels.

Then I decide to quit smoking.

Saturday, 4 February 2006

About once every fortnight I receive an email from someone or other who's convinced MI5 is secretly zapping him with a mind-controlling microwave weapon and can I investigate?

Today I email one of them back: 'For Christ's sake,' I write, 'MI5 haven't got the STAFF. They haven't even got enough people to sift through their AL-QAEDA PHONE TAP TRANSCRIPTS. They don't CARE about you and your slight anti-Government concerns, in your bloody house in BRECON. You think they're going to send someone to BRECON to ZAP YOU? From a TRANSIT VAN PARKED IN THE VILLAGE? THEY HAVEN'T GOT THE STAFF. GET OVER YOURSELF. Jon.'

It has been five days since I quit smoking.

Monday, 6 February 2006

My dedication to providing Joel with a constantly enchanting childhood has waned since I almost killed myself one night after he lost a tooth. I was leaning out of his window, attempting to fashion a fairy footprint out of glitter and glue on his windowsill. I nearly fell and died.

Just look at yourself, I thought.

Now, three years later, lots of people I know are moving their families out of London to the suburbs or the country. They buy houses with gardens and they get a family dog. And the child presumably spends its childhood running around the garden with the dog. Maybe there's a river at the bottom of their garden, and the child and the dog have rafting adventures.

Last week a friend, Alan, who is moving his family to the country, asked me what I believed were the advantages of raising a child in inner London.

'For a start, city children have a kind of sassy, street-smart wisdom,' I replied. 'And sarcasm. My son has developed an advanced sense of street-wise sarcasm.'

Alan gave me a look to say, 'The real reason why you're raising a child in London is that you're selfish. You're denying him a proper childhood – a rural childhood – because you like restaurants and cinemas. Whatever happened,' Alan's look continued, 'to the old days, when you'd do anything to enchant your child? Yes, you took it to idiotic lengths, but now you barely enchant him at all.'

It was a withering, complicated look he gave me.

Alan lives down the road from me, in Islington, although he will be gone by the end of the month. I looked around his house. He has the same bubble bath (L'Occitane), the same wall paint (Farrow and Ball off-white), the same kitchen wall clock, from After Noah, and on and on. It is chilling. He is my aesthetic doppelganger. I bet everyone around here has all this stuff too. I thought I'd been making random decisions all these years.

I'm looking after Joel. I put on the TV and go off upstairs to write emails. Joel watches a cartoon in which a father and son build a soapbox-derby racing car together. As a result they love each other more than ever.

'Dad,' Joel yells when it is over. 'Can we build a soapbox-derby racing car together?'

I bound into the room. 'Of *course* we can,' I emotionally yell.

'Really?' asks Joel.

'Let's do it!' I say.

'Great!' says Joel.

We can ask the neighbours to build them too, I think. We can go round, house to house, and get everyone into the idea. And get the council involved, close off some roads and get in bales of hay, and have a neighbourhood soapbox-derby race in the summer. The problem, I continue to think, is that it's all quite flat around here. The only street that's enough of a hill is Pentonville Road, and it's the main thoroughfare from the City to King's Cross. There's no way they'd close off Pentonville Road for us. I furrow my brow and think, The neighbours aren't going to all build soapbox-derby racing cars just because I ask them to. And I haven't got a clue how to build one. I don't even know if they're supposed to have *pedals*. There's no shame in that. I have different skills.

'Can we start building one now?' Joel asks.

If the impossible happened and I did manage to build one, I think, and they aren't supposed to have pedals, what the hell *then*? Joel would just sit in it? There are no hills around here other than Pentonville Road. That would be a pretty sad sight, wouldn't it? Joel all alone in a stationary soapbox-derby racing car, with uninvolved neighbours walking past him, pretending not to notice . . .

I grew up in a place called Lisvane in the suburbs of Cardiff. Every summer there was a huge soapbox-derby race. Everyone got involved. All the roads were closed off. There were different age categories. The winners got trophies. I couldn't wait to get out of Cardiff and move to London. Now I live in a place where even the thought of organizing a soapbox derby seems laughably idealistic.

Tuesday, 7 February 2006

Joel yells that I need to come and watch an advert on TV. It is for a dog-sponsoring charity. For £4 a month you can sponsor a dog called Tessa.

'Tessa has a fragile liver and so she is not allowed to eat too many treats,' the advert says.

We see Tessa, in the advert, walking around a field at a dog sanctuary somewhere. I'm not sure what breed Tessa is, but she has a head like a hammer.

'Can I sponsor Tessa?' Joel asks me.

'Of *course* you can,' I yell emotionally.

'I wonder if I'm allowed to give Tessa walks?' Joel

says. 'Do you think after we sponsor Tessa we can go and give her walks? Just once in a while?'

'I don't know,' I say. 'We'll have to check the terms and conditions once we've sponsored Tessa.'

'So we *can* sponsor Tessa?' Joel asks.

'Yes!' I say. 'Yes we can!'

'Thank you!' he says.

I pay the direct debit, and we wait for the paperwork.

Monday, 13 February 2006

I have to say I do not feel great about sponsoring Tessa. A few years ago I played in a charity poker game. The winner was to get £1,000 to donate to a charity of their choice. My £1,000 was to go to sick children. Midway through the game I went all in with tens. The then *Daily Express* columnist Carol Sarler called. She had aces. I was knocked out. Carol Sarler donated her £1,000 to Battersea Dogs Home. Nowadays, when I think back on that game, I imagine myself – a big, generous smile on my face – approaching sick children, my arms full of wonderful gifts. The sick children allow themselves small, hopeful smiles. And then, from nowhere, I am tripped to the ground by a cackling Carol Sarler, who snatches the gifts and scuttles off to give them to already overfed dogs.

I suppose it is unfair to imagine Carol Sarler – who I don't know – like this, but haven't dog charities got so much money they don't know what to do with it?

We receive our first letter from Tessa.

'I have a fragile liver so I'm not allowed to eat too many treats,' she writes. 'I love going for walks and being out in the fresh air. Paws truly, Tessa x.'

'Can we visit Tessa and take her for a walk?' Joel asks. 'Are we allowed?'

'I don't know,' I prevaricate.

Last week there was an article in the *Mail on Sunday*. It revealed that some people who believe they've sponsored goats in developing countries haven't. The goats don't actually exist, the article said, and the sponsorship money has gone to general agricultural initiatives instead. The *Mail on Sunday* made it sound like a big scandal, but I thought, Goats? General agricultural initiatives? What's the difference? Who cares?

But now – in the aftermath of us sponsoring Tessa – I cannot get the idea out of my head that Tessa might not be a real dog. She might instead be a figurative dog. Personally, I wouldn't care. My worry is, if we turn up in Bridgend might they bring out a dog that looks nothing like Tessa and say, 'This is Tessa?'

Thursday, 16 February 2006

Another letter arrives from Tessa. It is a belated Christmas card: 'Wishing you a very woofy Christmas. Tessa x.'

'I really want to visit Tessa,' Joel says.

I prevaricate again.

Monday, 20 February 2006

It costs £4 a month to sponsor Tessa, yet we seem to be getting more than £4 a month's worth of stuff sent back to us: Christmas cards, a Valentine's card, etc. Joel is thrilled, although a part of him wonders why he's getting quite so much stuff. For the first time in his life, he seems slightly turned off by what he perceives as neediness in another.

I telephone the rehoming centre and ask if we can visit Tessa next week, maybe Tuesday. Then I add, 'I bet all the other dogs are jealous of Tessa now she's a television celebrity!'

'I'll get the diary,' the receptionist says, slightly frostily.

Hang on, I think. You're the ones who started anthropomorphizing Tessa. I wouldn't have even *thought* to anthropomorphize her if it wasn't for that advert, and now your frosty silence makes it sound like you think I love dogs too much.

Tuesday, 28 February 2006

Tuesday. We're forty-five minutes late to meet Tessa. We're hopelessly lost in the system of roundabouts between the M4 and Bridgend. I can't get through to the rehoming centre for directions.

'I'm worried about Tessa,' yells Joel, distressed, from the back.

'*We'll never find it!*' I yell at Elaine.

'*Oh, Tessa!*' yells Joel, plaintively.

Elaine, who is equally tense, attempts to calm Joel by saying, 'It happens to *all* people who visit dogs.'

'What?' says Joel.

'It happens to *all* people who visit dogs,' Elaine repeats.

'What are you *talking* about?' says Joel.

'*Here* it is!' I say. We pull up. Tessa is waiting for us in the reception. She's recognizable from the advert, but with one very big difference. She is now heavily, shockingly muzzled. She rushes towards us, ferociously attempting to shake the muzzle from her face. Joel takes a terrified step backwards. Tessa goes for my penis, and the big brown muzzle smashes against it with the force of a cricket ball. I am practically thrown across the reception area.

'Are you going to thank Tessa for your Valentine's card, Joel?' I say. But I know there's no point.

'I'm disappointed by Tessa,' says Joel, back in the car, ten minutes later. We don't speak of her again.

Friday, 3 March 2006

I have some business in Bristol. Then we drive back to London. I've been looking for rural stop-offs to break up the journey – something lovely for children – and have settled on a demonstration of fudge-making at a village sweet shop in Cheddar.

'Imagine that!' I say to Joel as we pull off the M4. 'Imagine watching fudge being made! Like Willy Wonka!'

We arrive in the village, and park outside the sweet shop.

'Can you smell that?' I say. 'Mmmm.'

The demonstration has just begun. An audience of twenty are looking on. The fudge-maker has his back to the crowd. He's stirring something sweet-smelling in a big pot. I nudge Joel in the ribs and make an enchanted *Swallows and Amazons* type of cooing sound.

And then, still with his back to us, the fudge-maker begins to speak: 'Unfortunately, there are some sweet shops in Cheddar that sell fudge that was purchased last year and you can draw your own conclusions about that.'

He pauses and continues to mutter: 'We make real fudge here. Not like in those American fudge kitchens that use a pre-made mix. I'm sorry to disillusion you but that's *not* how fudge is made. It's how *fondant* is made.'

He is no Willy Wonka. He is barely even an Oompa-Loompa. There is, I realize, a disparity between how I'd like this man to be (twinkle-eyed, or at least willing to turn around) and how he actually *is* (clearly opposed to American fudge kitchens). How did it happen that city people have acquired the reputation for being surly and diffident? I'm forever smiling at tourists and suggesting they go to Tate Modern.

'Those of you that have visited the fudge kitchens in the States will know what I'm talking about,' he continues, more to himself than us. 'In the American fudge kitchens they might as well be mixing *paint*.'

I think I've identified the problem. He's assuming

we're the sorts of hardcore fudge enthusiasts who'll seek out fudge-making all over the world. In fact (and I think I can speak for the whole audience when I say this) we aren't here because of the fudge-making. We just want a little innocent countryside theme-parkish fun, with some free fudge-tasting thrown in.

'I'm afraid that's the interesting part of the demonstration over,' he announces, his back still to us. 'Now we wait for sixteen hours for the fudge to cool.'

'Thank you,' murmur one or two of the audience members, subdued and sad.

And we drive back to London, where we might indeed harbour a patronizingly metropolitan rose-tinted fantasy of village life, but at least we know how to put on a show for children.

Tuesday, 11 April 2006

Doug, a childhood friend of Elaine's, has come to visit us for lunch. Straight away he starts talking wistfully about the fantastic times they used to have together as teenagers. They stayed out all night and didn't have responsibilities like children or censorious husbands and wives who gave them a hard time if they had too much fun.

Doug shoots me a sideways glance as he says this. I furrow my brow and wonder whether Elaine told Doug, out of my earshot, that I give her a hard time if she stays out too late. For the next ten minutes I sit there, silently paranoid. Then, somehow, the conversation turns to the subject of the seven basic plots.

'Do you know about the seven basic plots?' Doug asks.

'No?' says Elaine.

'Yes!' I say.

In unison, Doug and I turn to Elaine.

'It's amazing,' I say. 'Every single plot *ever invented* falls into—'

One of seven categories!' interrupts Doug.

I scowl slightly at him.

'Writers all over the world have tried to come up with an *eighth plot*,' Doug continues, 'but they *just can't!*'

'I'm not sure that writers all over the world are actively trying to come up with an eighth plot,' I say, shooting Elaine a grin. 'Imagine – I don't know – Kazuo Ishiguro going, "I simply won't rest until I find that eighth basic plot!" Or imagine, let's say, John Updike, going—'

'Yeah, yeah,' interrupts Elaine. She knows that when I am in a sarcastic mood, bought on by what I perceive to be an injustice meted out by another in a social setting, I can be uncontrollably annoying, and it is her duty to stop this from happening.

'So,' she says. 'What *are* the seven basic plots?'

'Overcoming the monster,' I say. 'Um.'

'Ménage à trois,' says Doug.

'Ménage à trois isn't one of the seven basic plots,' I say.

'Yes, it is,' he says. 'Overcoming the monster. Ménage à trois. The older woman weaves her spell . . .'

'Just wait a minute,' I say. 'If ménage à trois is one of the seven basic plots, name me in quick succession—'

'Leave it, Jon,' says Elaine.

'No, no,' I say, waving her quiet. 'Name me, in quick succession, a number of stories that follow the ménage à trois template.'

'*Jules et Jim*,' says Doug. 'Uh . . .'

There is a silence.

'*Jules et Jim*?' I say. 'And . . . Oh! Maybe you can throw in a couple of older woman weaves her spell plots while you're at it. Let's think. *Basic Instinct 1. Basic Instinct 2.* The witch in *The Wizard of Oz* . . .'

Doug falls silent. He looks overcome.

'Coffee?' I say.

Wednesday, 12 April 2006

Six weeks ago, in the middle of a conversation with my wife shortly after watching *The Apprentice*, I suddenly and apropos of nothing said, 'You're a lightweight! Get out of this boardroom! You're fired!'

Elaine laughed.

'You're pathetic!' I said. 'You're fired!'

Elaine continued to laugh.

It's a catchphrase! I thought. I have *identified* a catchphrase!

For a moment I wondered whether other people were going around saying, 'You're fired!' But I concluded that nobody else was. If they were, someone would have said it to me, or I would have overheard someone say it.

For the next week or two, I said, 'You're fired!' to Elaine and Joel whenever the opportunity arose, much to their delight. Giddy with success I even – and this is unlike me – gave it a try on a few occasions beyond the safety of the immediate family. We had friends round one Sunday, and I said to them, midway through lunch, 'You're fired!'

They groaned theatrically and laughed.

I also did it over a business lunch with people I barely knew.

'Get out of this boardroom!' I said. 'Get down to the market. Buy me some fruit and veg. Or you're fired!' They laughed politely.

I grinned as if to say, 'See how I've identified this as a whole new catchphrase!'

They grinned back although, being lost in the moment, I failed to see that their grins were thin at best.

There's a scene in the movie *See No Evil* in which the blind Mia Farrow is wandering around her uncle's remote farmhouse unaware that her entire family has been grotesquely murdered, and that there is carnage everywhere. For ages she wanders around, missing corpses by inches. Then, suddenly, she brushes up against a mutilated body, screams, runs blindly backwards into another mutilated body, screams again, falls into the bloody lap of a third corpse and so on. This is what happens to me today regarding the realization that going around saying, 'You're fired!' is in fact an idiotic cliché.

I watch Charlie Brooker on TV saying anyone who thinks it's funny to say, 'You're fired!' in the style of Sir Alan Sugar is a twat.

Huh? I think. An hour later, I overhear someone on the Tube say to someone, 'He's such an idiot. He goes around doing those stupid Sir Alan Sugar catchphrases.' I furrow my brow. How could I have missed this?

Tuesday, 18 April 2006

I'm at the home of the hypnotist Paul McKenna. We're chatting away about how some people are inclined to replace rational fears with irrational ones.

'It's like my son,' I say. 'He's worried that bears will invade the house yet he doesn't look left and right when he's crossing the road.'

'Exactly!' says Paul McKenna. 'More people are killed by donkeys than by airplanes, yet nobody has donkey phobias.'

'Exactly!' I say.

What a lovely man, I think. I'm here to interview him, but I can imagine myself becoming good friends with him. I wonder if I should invite him out for a meal or something. I have a mental picture of the two of us in a restaurant throwing our heads back and laughing. But then I think, No. I'm only a journalist to him. Ah well.

Three days pass. I'm having supper with Elaine.

'Isn't it funny,' I muse out loud, 'that more people are killed by donkeys than by airplanes.'

Elaine looks up from her plate. 'That's rubbish,' she says. 'Who told you that?'

There's a silence. 'Paul McKenna,' I say.

'Well, it's total bollocks,' she says.

'Paul McKenna would have no reason to lie,' I say, defiantly.

'Well, *think* about it,' she says.

'Obviously fewer people were killed by donkeys than by airplanes in 2001,' I say. 'But I'm sure it's true generally speaking.'

'Look it up on Google if you're so sure of yourself,' says Elaine, sarcastically.

But I don't want to. A good person wouldn't cross-check on Google what a friend says to them in small talk. Yes, people are fallible. There's a possibility Paul McKenna made it up on the spot, just for something interesting to say, but only a censorious monster would delight in opening *that* Pandora's box. I tell Elaine that, and she replies that I *am* that censorious monster.

'I *used* to be,' I say. '*Used* to be.'

'You still are,' she says. 'You're just defending him because he's Famous Paul McKenna.'

'*OK*,' I snarl. 'I'll *look it up on Google*.'

'This statement has been plaguing us for several years,' writes the American Donkey and Mule Society. 'It is *totally false*. In Nov 2005 we found *one* headline of a man in Egypt being killed by his donkey, but in truth more people are bitten by their family dog! Help us to dispel this awful rumour-mill factoid.'

'See?' says Elaine in my ear. 'It *was* rubbish.'

'Yes,' I say, 'but Paul McKenna's no fantasist. That's the important thing. He's a good man proved wrong on this one point. He believed an urban legend. There's no shame in that.'

No shame at all, I think.

PART TWO

6. PHONING A FRIEND

In November 2001, when Major Charles Ingram, his wife Diana and another man, Tecwen Whittock, were arrested attempting to cheat the TV show *Who Wants To Be A Millionaire?* out of a million pounds using an elaborate system of audience-based coughs, my mother called me to say, 'You know them! You were at school with them!'

'With who?' I asked.

'Diana Ingram's brothers, Adrian and Marcus Pollock,' she said. 'You must remember Diana Pollock. Their cousin Julian lived around the corner from us. You must remember them.'

'No,' I said.

The next day it dawned on me that this was an in that money couldn't buy, so I wrote to the Ingrams, reminding them of our halcyon days together.

'My family and I are experiencing a very real nightmare,' Charles wrote back. 'I have no doubt that there is a case to prove against media manipulation after consideration of the content, its cyclical nature, the care taken to quickly undermine expressions of support, the outrageous leaking of privileged information, and so on.'

Charles wrote that perhaps I was the journalist to prove that case. I reread the letter. Its cyclical nature? It seemed curiously over-erudite, as if Charles wanted to prove that he was the sort of person clever enough to legitimately win £1m. I had no idea what he meant.

Still, it was odd. Diana, Adrian and Marcus Pollock attended the same synagogue I did. They were well-to-do in an ordinary way. What happened to them? I did, in fact, have some vague memory, some Pollock-related to-do that rocked the local Jewish community when I was about ten. It was something to do with a car with the number plate APOLLO G and the manufacture of watch straps. But I couldn't remember anything more than that, and neither could my mother. I decided to attend the trial at Southwark Crown Court. Midway through, however, I was struck by another mystery. Why was this silly trial – in which almost everyone involved seemed to have their own crazy get-rich-quick scheme – happening at all?

Thursday afternoon, 20 March 2003, is when it all goes wrong for Charles Ingram. He's being cross-examined by prosecuting barrister Nicholas Hilliard about Particular Coughs 12 to 14. Those of us who've attended this long, slow trial from the beginning know the coughs so well we can mouth them: the tape of Charles's appearance on *Millionaire* has been played nearly a dozen times. During Charles's tenure in the hot seat, 192 coughs rang out from the audience: 173 were, experts agree, innocent clearings of throats, etc. But 19 have been termed Particular Coughs.

Perhaps the most devastating of all is Particular Cough 12. It arose during Chris Tarrant's £500,000 question: 'Baron Haussmann is best known for his planning of which city? Rome, Paris, Berlin, Athens.'

'I think it's Berlin,' Charles immediately, and confidently, replied. 'Haussmann is a more German name than Italian or Parisian or Athens. I'd be saying Berlin if I was at home watching this on TV.'

This is when Cough 12 occurred. It sounds, from the tape, like a cough born from terrible frustration. If the prosecution case is true, the plan was for Charles to chew over the answers out loud and for Tecwen Whittock – sitting behind him in a Fastest Finger First seat – to cough after the correct one. But now it seemed that Charles was going to plump straight for Berlin.

'Cough, NO!'

(The first time this 'No!' was played in court, every journalist and member of the public burst out laughing. Judge Rivlin threatened to clear the court.)

'I don't think it's Paris,' he said.

'Cough.'

'I don't think it's Athens.'

No cough.

'I'm sure it's not Rome.'

No cough.

'I would have thought it's Berlin but there's a chance it's Paris,' said Charles. 'Think, think! I think it's Berlin. It could be Paris. I think it's Paris.'

'Cough.'

'Yes,' said Charles. 'I am going to play . . .'

Now Nicholas Hilliard asks Charles why he changed his mind and opted for Paris.

'I knew that Paris was a planned city,' explains Charles. 'The centre of Paris was cleared of slums during the nineteenth century, and it was rebuilt into districts and boulevards. Prominent in my mind was the economic reason. In the middle of the nineteenth century France was coming out of the revolutionary period and it was decided, I think by Napoleon III, that he would concentrate on Paris and thereby the remainder of France would flourish.'

Charles looks hopefully at the jury.

'But at the time,' sighs Hilliard, 'you said you thought it was Berlin because he had a German-sounding name.'

There is a silence.

'Oh, Mr Ingram,' says Hilliard. 'Surely you can help us a little bit better than that.'

Judge Rivlin calls for a break. We all file out to the corridor. Charles looks shaken. He lights a cigarillo, his face beetroot and a picture of self-loathing. Nobody notices that he's wearing a Mensa badge. He put it on as a special touch, but it is so tiny – just a little M on his lapel – that the jury can't spot it.

'Hilliard has got me all tied up in knots,' he says. 'I just don't want to say anything stupid.'

I do an upbeat smile, even though I believe that only a miracle can save them now.

'How does it feel to have to keep watching that tape?' I ask. I imagine it must be embarrassing. From the tape they look quite extraordinarily guilty, albeit in a sweet and funny way. It seems such a slapstick-type crime – a half-baked plot executed badly.

'I still get a thrill,' Charles replies, 'when it gets to the part where I win a million.'

Corridors outside courtrooms are exciting places. The players all stand together smoking cigarettes – defendants, barristers, clerks, ushers, solicitors, journalists, police and victims – as if there's a victim in this crime! Celador, the makers of *Millionaire*, have signed up almost every witness for a documentary to be shown across the world after the verdict. This will, of course, earn them far more than the £1m they say Charles almost cheated out of them. Sometimes I think that whoever masterminded this harebrained plot should be given a cut of Celador's documentary profits. I wonder who the criminal genius was. I don't think it was Charles.

The only major players who've not been signed up by Celador are the defendants. Three thousand journalists have approached the Ingrams for interviews. Although I am way ahead, being a family friend, I note that many other reporters have their own ingratiating tactics, and I'm not resting on my laurels. On Day One, for example, Charles entered court and gave his solicitors a kind of victory salute: a punch in the air. Half a dozen journalists, me included, thought he was punching the air at us, so we performed slightly awkward victory salutes back. It was a little embarrassing.

A few feet down the corridor, the reporters gather in a circle, comparing notes.

'I liked it when Charles said the charges were "absolute rot",' says one journalist.

'Do you think we can get away with having him say "tommyrot"?' says another. Everyone laughs.

It is agreed that Hilliard is a brilliantly scathing cross-examiner. A passing barrister – on his way to Court 5 – tells me that Hilliard 'trounced me in a murder trial once'. I didn't think to ask him whether the convicted murderer did it or not.

Tecwen Whittock sits far down the corridor, sometimes alone, sometimes with his son, Rhys. He's so unassuming that I never once see him enter the dock. He just seems to materialize. I wander over to him.

'I'm from Cardiff, too,' I say.

'That's a coincidence,' he says.

'And my mother went to Howell's,' I say.

Howell's is the private school Tecwen sent his daughter to, running up a £20,000 bill. This debt, say the prosecutors, was Tecwen's motive.

'See?' says Tecwen. 'That's another coincidence. Coincidences do happen!'

'I was at prep school with Adrian and Marcus Pollock,' I say.

'That's another coincidence!' says Tecwen. 'I'd like to see what Hilliard would do to you, with all those coincidences, if he got you on the stand.'

I don't tell Tecwen the fourth coincidence – that Judge Rivlin is a distant cousin of my mother's.

I wander down the corridor to talk to the arresting officers. 'Is this trial really worth it?' I ask Detective Sergeant Ian Williamson. 'I mean, come on, in the end, what exactly did they do? Why didn't Celador just settle their differences with the Ingrams in a civil court?'

This is the worst question you can ask an arresting officer. They hate ambiguities. The police have a lot to lose if this trial goes badly for them. Some of the arresting officers were Paul Burrell's arresting officers. They really need a success after that fiasco.

'This trial,' Williamson replies, crisply, 'is about protecting the integrity of the *Millionaire* format. *Millionaire* is the most popular quiz show in the history of television. Celador has sold it to a hundred countries. Thousands of jobs depend on its success . . .'

This is true. In fact, a BBC reporter down the corridor has just returned from Jordan, where she was meeting Palestinian leaders. They asked her why she was going back to Britain. 'It's to do with a quiz show called *Who Wants To Be A Millionaire?*,' she said. The Palestinian leaders got really excited and said, 'The Coughing Major! You're going to that trial?'

So I understand what Williamson means, but another thought occurs to me. The prize money Charles allegedly tried to cheat out of Celador came from the revenue generated from the premium-rate phone lines – the calls the viewers make in their frequently fruitless attempts to get on to the show. So it is revenue generated from the far-fetched hopes and dreams of the viewing public, which seems like a cheat in itself. And how much is this trial costing? The answer is around £1m. If there's a guilty verdict, we the viewing public stand to lose £1m. If there's a not-guilty verdict, and Celador are forced to give Charles his cheque back, we will lose £2m.

'Watching that cross-examination has taught me one thing,' I say to DS Williamson. 'If I'm ever in a situation like that, I'm going to plead guilty.'

There is a small silence.

'Proper criminals do,' he replies.

Every morning sees a scrum for the public-gallery seats. I secure my place each day because, like a weirdo, I arrive an hour early and I don't budge, even though I often very much need the toilet. Charles's father, himself an army man, sits next to me. He wears a tiepin shaped like a steam train. Unyielding pensioners with flasks of coffee mercilessly nab most of the other seats. One regular keeps passing me notes. I tend to open them with great anticipation. It is exciting to be handed a note in a courtroom. Today's note reads: 'Is your suit made out of corduroy?'

The pensioners spend much of the day noisily unwrapping packets of Lockets and readjusting their screeching hearing aids. A young man behind me cracks his knuckles from 10 a.m. to 4 p.m. Each time the barristers mention the word 'cough' – and the word 'cough' is mentioned very frequently – many people sitting around me involuntarily cough. We are like a comedy-club audience, determined to enjoy ourselves even if the comedian isn't very funny. Even Chris Tarrant's reading of the oath gets a loud chuckle from a man behind me.

Chris Tarrant may not be the world's greatest superstar, but within the context of this grubby building we've come to call home, the wallpaper peeling, the soap in the toilets as hard as rock, the evidence dragging on and on, he is like a vision of paradise entering Court 4. Everyone is smitten.

'Has anyone ever got the first question wrong?' asks one defence barrister.

'It's happened in America,' replies Tarrant, to huge laughter around the court. Tarrant looks surprised. He was just giving a factual response. During all the merriment, the fact that Tarrant heard no coughing, suspected no foul play and even said to the show's producers, 'Don't be stupid,' when he was told of their suspicions, seems to have got lost.

Rod Taylor, Celador's head of marketing, gets a big laugh, too, during his evidence about how he frisked Charles shortly after he'd 'won' the million. Taylor offers to frisk one of the barristers to show him how he did it. That gets a laugh. In the dock, Charles begins to cry.

'Why then?' I ask him at Starbucks the next day. 'Why did you cry at that moment?'

I often meet Charles and Diana at Starbucks. I discovered early on that if I happen to be there at 9.05 a.m., this is exactly when Charles queues up. We make small talk. Five minutes a day. That adds up, in my reckoning, to a substantial exclusive interview.

'It was when Mr Aubrey [Tecwen Whittock's barrister] was cross-examining Rod Taylor and he said something and everyone laughed,' replies Charles.

'What did he say?' I ask.

'He made a joke,' says Charles. 'Here I am, this cataclysmic event, my family on the line, and everyone is laughing. And you know how I feel about not wanting to look stupid.'

'What was the joke?' I ask. 'What was the exact thing he said that made you cry?'

Charles pauses. Then he says, 'It was when Mr Aubrey said to Rod Taylor, "Did you search his privates?" '

This story begins in 2000. Tecwen Whittock was watching *Who Wants To Be A Millionaire?* one night when he recognized a contestant, but couldn't remember where from. I could have told him. It was my old school pal, Diana's brother, Adrian Pollock.

That's the same guy, Tecwen realized, who was on a few weeks ago. He's been on four times now! I think I'll track him down and ask him what his secret is.

Tecwen is a quiz-show veteran. He keeps a journal of trivia, of random facts and figures accrued over the years. He's been on *15–1*, although he was eliminated in the first round. He didn't fare much better on *The People Versus* . . . He managed to Beat the Bong, whatever that means, but still only won £500. *Sale of the Century* was another disaster. 'I convinced my wife I'd win a car, but in fact I won the booby prize of a world atlas,' he later tells the court. He had, however, once made it to the semi-final of *Brain of Britain*.

Tecwen hoped to buy a silk bed for his dog, Bouncer, and a Robin Reliant for his son, Rhys, who was a member of the *Only Fools and Horses* fan club and wanted to drive the same car as the Trotters. Plus, he had credit-card debts from his children's private education. He wondered if Adrian Pollock might give him tips on becoming a contestant, so he tracked him down to St Hilary, a village near Cardiff, and staked out his home.

'He seemed normal,' Tecwen later told the police. 'A couple of kids. A dog.'

When he later read that he and Marcus were supposedly involved in some Internet scam, he thought, 'Uh oh. Suspicious.'

Tecwen introduced himself to Adrian, who was flattered by his curiosity. They went to the pub, where Adrian took on the role of Tecwen's mentor, imparting his secrets. First, Adrian told Tecwen, keep calling Celador's premium-rate phone line. Adrian had himself phoned 1,700 times. Second, when the random selector asks you a trivia question, try and answer it in a computer voice. Adrian had come to believe that Celador had programmed the selector to weed out certain regional accents.

He took his mentoring of Tecwen very seriously. He and Marcus visited Tecwen's home. They spoke on the phone twenty-seven times. Adrian even asked Diana to become Tecwen's co-mentor.

'What did you talk to him about?' asks Hilliard, when he cross-examines Diana about her relationship with Tecwen.

'The Closest-To question,' replies Diana.

The 'Closest-To' is the question the *Millionaire* researchers ask you over the phone if you've been randomly selected and are now down to the last hundred possible contestants. It is always a numerical question: 'How many radio stations are there in North America?' for example.

'They can be quite hard,' explains Diana. 'They've always got a numerical answer that could be anything, really.'

'And that's the kind of insight you were offering Tecwen Whittock, was it?' asks Hilliard. 'That they're quite hard and could be anything really?'

In fact, shortly before the arrests, Adrian and Diana delivered a manuscript of a book to John Brown Publishing, offering tips on how to get on to *Millionaire*. Both Diana and Adrian had won £32,000 in the hot seat. John Brown was ready to publish, but the arrests changed all that.

Meanwhile, over in Devizes, Wiltshire, Adrian had loaned his brother-in-law, Charles, his pretend mock-up Fastest Finger First console. Charles practised being fast-fingered on it. He phoned and phoned the random selector. He didn't, however, imitate a staccato computer voice. He thought Adrian's conspiracy theory about that was far-fetched. In fact, he later tells the court, he really doesn't like Adrian and Marcus.

'I don't like Diana getting involved in whatever it is they do,' he says, adding that Adrian and Marcus have a history of getting involved in harebrained get-rich-quick schemes.

Back in Cardiff, Tecwen repeatedly called the *Million-*

aire random selector in a staccato voice. 'Before I knew it,' he tells the court, 'it worked. I was on.'

Tecwen was booked to appear on 10 September 2001. Charles got on, too – on 9 September. Even though the prosecution says that some other plot was probably in operation that evening, involving buzzing pagers strapped to Charles's body, or perhaps to Marcus's body, sitting in the audience, Charles didn't do well. He made it to £4,000 but lost two of his lifelines before the recording ended. Still, he survived to carry on the following night. Chris Tarrant announced the names of the Fastest Finger contestants who'd be joining Charles in the studio. Second on the list was Tecwen Whittock.

Charles told the police that the first he'd heard of Tecwen Whittock was two weeks later, on 25 September, when the *Sun* named him as the mysterious cougher. He says the first time he met him was just a few weeks ago, right here at Southwark Crown Court. Certainly, in the dock, they studiously behave as if they are strangers. However, Diana's mobile telephone bill shows that at 11.02 p.m. on the night of 9 September – as the Ingrams were driving home from the studio down the M4 – she phoned Tecwen for just over five minutes. Diana says the call was simply to congratulate her fellow

Millionaire devotee on getting on to the show, and that Charles was asleep at the time. The prosecution says the call was for the three of them to put the coughing plot into action, a plot that must have been vaguely hatched during the 'mentoring' conversations of the previous weeks.

When DS Williamson told me a few days ago that 'proper criminals' plead guilty, I asked him what made the Ingrams and Tecwen not proper criminals. He said, 'They may have engaged in a criminal act, but they don't have criminal minds. They made too many stupid mistakes.'

One stupid mistake, he said, was that they called each other on their own phones. Another was that, at the *Millionaire* studio on 10 September, neither Charles nor Diana said a word to Tecwen. How suspicious for Diana 'the mentor' not to say hello to her student, especially when they'd been on the phone with each other just hours earlier. Diana says she didn't talk to Tecwen because she didn't know what he looked like. The most stupid mistake of all – say the police – was that they made it so bloody obvious.

The audience gave Charles a standing ovation after he correctly answered the £1m question. Diana ran down the studio stairs to hug her husband. Her radio microphone picked up her saying, 'How the hell did you do it?

You must be mad!' As they walked to their dressing room, another Fastest Finger contestant congratulated them and said, 'How did you get the Holbein question?' Diana turned to Charles, 'Oh, that was one you knew, wasn't it, darling?'

Chris Tarrant: '*The Ambassadors* in the National Gallery is a painting by which artist: Van Eyck? Holbein? Michelangelo? Rembrandt?'

Charles: 'I think it was either Holbein or Rembrandt. I've seen it. I think it was Holbein.'

'Cough.'

Charles: 'I'm sure it was Holbein.'

'Cough.'

Charles: 'I'm sure it was Holbein. I'm sure of it. I think I'm going to go for it.'

'Cough.'

Charles: 'Yeah, Holbein.'

Chris Tarrant: 'You're fantastic, just fantastic.'

It is week three of the trial, and the Ingrams' case has been effortlessly torn apart by Nicholas Hilliard.

'It's not nice to watch, is it?' says one arresting officer to me out in the corridor. I'm starting to think it may be driving Charles towards some sort of breakdown. He's already told the court about his year on medication since the arrest, how passers-by yell 'Cheat!' when he's in his garden having a picnic and how someone recently tried

181

to shoot his cat, though this may have been unconnected. Personally, I think being cross-examined by Hilliard is punishment enough for a bit of cheeky deception on *Millionaire*.

My relationship with Charles is becoming awkward. My upbeat smiles have involuntarily turned into pitying grimaces. Charles seems compelled to behave in a fake-laddish manner in front of me.

'Oh,' he laughs throatily in the corridor in a break after performing particularly badly on cross-examination, 'I knew I shouldn't have gone out on the piss last night!'

I play along. 'Did you?' I ask.

'Well,' he adds, theatrically massaging his forehead, 'it was a supper party, but it was much the same thing!'

'Charles!' calls Diana from down the corridor. 'Come here!'

'Sorry, sorry,' he calls back.

Diana has gone off me. Yesterday I was staring into space for a long time near Starbucks, thinking about other things, when I realized that I was staring straight at Diana, who was looking back at me, horrified, as if I was an obsessed stalker glaring at her from afar.

Today an incongruously suave stranger sits next to me in the public gallery. He is Robert Brydges, and he was in the *Millionaire* audience on 10 September.

'I kept looking round for where Charles was getting

help from,' Robert says. 'I knew the process was bogus – he was just so erratic – but I didn't hear the coughs.'

Robert thinks Charles should have stuck on £500,000. Celador might have been suspicious, but it would have probably honoured the cheque. Even though Robert himself was suspicious, he was also inspired by Charles's success. Over the next two days, while Britain reeled from the World Trade Centre attacks, Robert repeatedly called the *Millionaire* random selector.

'I worked out,' he says, 'that if you call three hundred and fifty times you have a fifty–fifty chance of getting on to a particular show.'

He phoned more than a thousand times.

'I read that Charles had been practising the Fastest Finger First on a mock-up console, so I built one, too, on my laptop.'

Robert's plan worked. On 25 September, he found himself in the same place Charles had been a fortnight earlier – in the *Millionaire* hot seat.

The next day's *Sun* headline read: 'MILLIONAIRE WORTH FEW BOB MORE'.

Super-rich Robert Brydges beamed with joy last night as he returned home after winning a million on *Who Wants To Be A Millionaire?*. Banker Robert could not contain his excitement, even though he was a millionaire twice over *before* appearing on the quiz show. He declared with a grin: "Believe me I'm happy. I'm very happy."

Robert is writing a book called *The Third Millionaire* about his and Charles's parallel lives. What is it about the human condition that one good man can win £1m legitimately, when another has to resort to fraud? In the corridor, Robert introduces himself to Charles and mentions the name of his book.

'If you don't mind, I like to think of you as the fourth millionaire,' says Charles.

'Can we agree on 3A and 3B?' says Robert.

'Charles!' calls Diana, from down the corridor.

'OK, sorry!' Charles calls back, and scuttles off.

'I don't care how many Mensa badges he's wearing,' mutters Robert. 'On the £8,000 question he could hardly remember that Emmental cheese was from Switzerland.'

I laugh.

'Does all this remind you of Macbeth?' says Robert. 'The bluff soldier, with the pale, mysterious woman behind him?'

We regulars spend much of our time psychoanalysing the Ingrams. This is because their demeanours are so uncriminal. Even the police, unusually, get involved in the speculation.

'The major is a strange character,' says one arresting officer during a press briefing. 'Puzzling. I can't figure him out. There have been some comments in court about Diana being stronger . . .' He pauses. 'I don't understand that sort of relationship. I'm not part of a relationship like that.'

'You're a lucky man!' shouts a journalist.

At 2.15 p.m. on 23 March, a miracle occurs that might just save the defendants. Tecwen Whittock takes the stand, and he is brilliant. He begins with a tour of his harrowing childhood: born in a psychiatric hospital to a mother with behavioural problems, whom he never saw again, and an alcoholic father he never knew.

'I have a recollection of seeing him once when I was seven,' he says.

He was raised in foster care, and pulled himself up through hard work to become Head of Business Studies at Pontypridd Polytechnic.

'Would you jeopardize all you've worked for to get involved in something like this?' asks his barrister, David Aubrey.

'Of course not,' says Tecwen. 'I wouldn't do that. It's against all my morals, all I do. I wouldn't put my family on the line for this. I know I'd land up in jail.' It is a convincing moment. And then comes the bombshell. Look closely at the photograph, says David Aubrey – it was a long-lens photograph of Tecwen on his way to work, head bowed, that appeared in the *Sun* on 25 September.

'What have you got in your hand in that photograph?' asks David Aubrey.

'Some work files,' replies Tecwen.

'And in your other hand?'

'Two 500ml bottles.'

'Bottles of what?'

'Water. Tap water.'

And then it all comes flooding out. Tecwen has his entire life suffered from a persistent cough. Water helps. He carries some everywhere, and fruit juice, and inhalers and cough medicine. It's a ticklish cough, like a frog in his throat, very phlegmy. A stream of doctors and friends take the stand, attesting to Tecwen's irritating cough.

Aubrey sums up by saying, 'So, when was this plan supposedly hatched? During a late-night telephone call, on 9 September, lasting less than five minutes. Is it really likely that Mr Whittock would take part in such a hastily conceived scheme? Wouldn't he have said, "You can't count on me. I'm liable to cough at any time!"'

My relationship with the Ingrams has suffered a dreadful blow. Not only does Diana think I glower at her with a crazed expression, but the Ingrams have now appointed a media agent called David Thomas. These days, every time I bump into them at Starbucks or in the corridor outside Court 4, Thomas is there, saying, 'Hello, Jon,' in a snarly manner. The rumour is that Thomas is going to hand-pick one journalist, and the rest of us will get nothing.

'Can I have just five minutes with the Ingrams?' I ask him.

'I'm mentally logging your request,' says Thomas.

'All I want is for them to be able to tell their side of the story,' I say.

'So your pitch is "I'm Honest Jon",' he replies.

'Yes.'

'It's mentally logged,' says Thomas. 'You've batted your corner very well.'

I tell him my one question: 'What was that thing that happened back in our childhoods with the watch straps and the number plate APOLLO G?'

'Your question is logged up here,' he says, pointing at his head. I spend the next three days sitting in the corridor waiting for him to come back with an answer.

The jury retires to consider their verdict, and the corridor outside Court 4 becomes a frenzied bazaar. While everyone else crowds around Thomas, telling him how much they love dogs, too (Thomas is a dog lover), and explaining that all they want to do is let the Ingrams tell their side of the story (he tells them they batted their corners well), I sidle up to Diana.

'I'll tell you the one thing I really want to know . . .' I begin breezily.

'Have you met David Thomas?' she replies, looking frantically around for him.

Robert Brydges hears that John Brown Publishing – the company that had once planned to publish Diana and Adrian's book – is now interested in reading the manuscript of *The Third Millionaire*.

Suddenly, there is drama. Judge Rivlin calls us all back in. 'A very serious matter has arisen that does not concern the defendants,' he says. The jury is temporarily discharged. We file back out into the corridor, bewildered. It turns out that a juror was overheard holding court in a pub, saying how fantastic it was to be on the *Millionaire* trial jury. For a day and a half, the various parties debate whether to start the trial again with a new jury. In the end, Judge Rivlin decides to allow the eleven remaining jurors to continue.

'Well, that,' Charles mutters to himself, 'amounted to the square root of fuck-all.'

So this trial, which was all about entertainment, is almost chucked out because one of the jurors found it too entertaining.

When the guilty verdict comes in, after nearly fourteen

hours of deliberations over three days, Diana closes her eyes and looks down. Charles holds her hand and kisses her on the cheek. Tecwen doesn't respond in any way. The only noises in court are tuts – the kind of tuts that mean 'it's all a bit of a shame'.

Charles and Diana have three daughters, two with special needs.

Judge Rivlin has the reputation of being tough when sentencing, but says, 'I'm going to put you out of your misery. There's no way I'm going to deprive these children of their parents.'

The defence barristers stand up to make their mitigation pleas. In the public gallery the defendants' family members strain to hear what's being said. We can just make out, 'His career in the army is at an end . . . their home was provided by the army, so they've lost their home . . . the children are suffering from panic attacks . . . all three will have to leave their schools . . .'

The reason why we can only barely hear this is because three pensioners in the public gallery are coughing uncontrollably.

Judge Rivlin says it was all just a shabby schoolboy trick. He says he doesn't think this crime was about greed, it was about wanting to look good on a TV quiz show. He says the fact that their reputations have been so publicly ruined is appropriate punishment – and I remember what Charles said about how he hates to be thought of as stupid. Judge Rivlin hands out suspended sentences and fines totalling £60,000. On the courthouse steps, the paparazzi cough theatrically when Tecwen and his quiet son Rhys walk out.

The scrum is even more dramatic for Charles and Diana. Cameras and tripods and photographers crash to the floor in the violent scuffle to get pictures. 'I've seen child murderers get more respect than that,' says one journalist. Other journalists and some nearby builders scream with laughter at Charles and Diana and chant, 'Cheat! Cheat! Cheat!'

I phone David Thomas to ask if Diana can give me the answer to my question. He says, 'You've not fallen off my mental list.' I never hear from him again.

Instead I phone childhood friends to ask if they can remember anything about it. Most of them can. There were two Pollock brothers, they tell me. Bill and Arthur. They were in a family business together, making leather watch straps. There was a big falling out in the family, and Arthur left the company. Bill became rich, driving around in a fancy car with the personalized number plate APOLLO G. His family were the ones who lived near me, in a big house in Lisvane. They had a son called Julian. Arthur Pollock never really recovered. He was left penniless and in ill-health. His children vowed to pull themselves back up, and never suffer the indignity their father endured. They would make something of their lives, they promised themselves. So Adrian and Marcus set up an estate agency together, and Diana married an army major. The estate agency failed. In fact, the whole thing failed.

7. THE FALL OF A POP IMPRESARIO

10 September 2001. The Old Bailey trial of the pop mogul and former pop star Jonathan King, in which he is accused of a series of child-sex offences dating back to the sixties, seventies and eighties, begins this morning. Back in July, Judge Paget decided, for the purposes of case management, to have three trials instead of one. So the jury will hear only the charges that relate to the years between 1982 and 1987. There are six within this time frame – one buggery, one attempted buggery and four indecent assaults on boys aged fourteen and fifteen.

I have been having an email correspondence with Jonathan King for the past nine months, and last night he emailed me to say, 'I think you know, young Ronson, that whichever way it goes for me you could have an award-winning story here, if you're brave. You can change the face of Great Britain if you do it well. Good luck! JK.'

I have just returned from New York, and in the

canteen on the third floor of the Old Bailey – in the minutes before the trial is due to begin – Jonathan King comes over to make small talk about my trip.

'Did you bring me any presents back?' he asks. 'Any small boys? Just kidding! Don't you think it is amazing that I have retained my sense of humour?'

He smiles across the canteen at his arresting officers. They smile faintly back. Jonathan has always told me about his good relationship with the police, how kind they were to him during his arrest, and he looks a little crestfallen at their evident withdrawal of affection.

'The police are far less friendly than they were,' he says. 'Quite boot-faced, in fact.' He pauses. 'And there doesn't even seem to be a senior officer around. I'm getting quite insulted that I'm so unimportant that only constables are allowed anywhere near the case.'

He looks at me for a response. What should I say? Yes, his crimes are so significant and he is so famous that it would seem appropriate for a more senior officer to be in attendance? In the end, I just shrug.

There are half a dozen journalists here today covering the case. In the lobby outside the court, Jonathan approaches some to shake their hands. 'Who's the gorgeous blonde with a TV cameraman?' he whispers to me. 'Sorry if this ruins my image.'

'I felt terrible about shaking his hand,' one reporter

says a little later. 'I felt disgusting. I was standing there thinking, "What's he done with that hand?" I should have refused to shake it.'

'I just asked my solicitor if it's unusual for the accused to make a point of shaking the hands of the press and the prosecution barrister,' Jonathan says as we walk into court. 'He said it was absolutely unheard of!' Jonathan laughs, and adds, 'You know, I fully intend to change the legal system just like I changed the pop industry.'

And, at that, we take our seats. The jury is selected, and the trial begins.

On 24 November 2000, Jonathan King was charged with three child-sex offences, dating back thirty-two years. In the light of the publicity surrounding his arrest, a dozen other boys (now men) came forward to tell police that King had abused them too, during the seventies and eighties. Some said he picked them up at the Walton Hop, a disco in Walton-on-Thames run by his friend Deniz Corday. Others said he cruised them in his Rolls-Royce in London. He'd pull over and ask why they were out so late and did they know who he was. He was Jonathan King! Did they want a lift?

He told the boys he was conducting market research into the tastes of young people. Did they like his music? His TV shows? Were they fans of *Entertainment USA*, his BBC2 series? He asked them to complete a questionnaire – written by him – to list their hobbies in order of preference. Cars? Music? Family and friends? Sex?

'Oh, really?' Jonathan would say to them. 'You've only put sex at number two?'

And so they would get talking about sex. He sometimes took them to his Bayswater mews house, with its mirrored toilet and casually scattered photos of naked women on the coffee table. Sometimes, he took them to car parks, or to the forests near the Walton Hop. He showed them photographs of naked Colombian air hostesses and Sam Fox. He could, he said, arrange for them to have sex with the women in the photos.

Sometimes, within the bundle of photographs of naked women he would hand the boys, there would be a picture of himself naked. 'Oh!' he'd say, blushing a little. 'Sorry. You weren't supposed to see that one of me!' (When the police raided King's house, they say they found ten overnight bags, each stuffed with his seduction kit – his questionnaires and photos of Sam Fox and photos of himself naked – all packed and ready for when the urge took him to get into his Rolls-Royce and start driving around.)

He told the boys that it was fine if they wanted to masturbate. And then things would progress from there. Some of the boys reported that his whole body would start to shake as he sat next to them in the Rolls-Royce.

And then he 'went for it', in the words of one victim. None of the boys say that he forced himself onto them. They all say they just sat there, awed by his celebrity. The boys all say that Jonathan King has emotionally scarred them for life, although almost all of them returned, on many occasions, and became the victims of more assaults.

Later, Jonathan King will spend his last weekend of freedom – the weekend before the guilty verdicts – recording for me a video diary of his feelings about the charges. At one point, midway through this twenty-minute tape, he hollers into the camera about this perplexing aspect of the case. 'They kept coming back to me again and again and again, although this vile behaviour was supposed to be taking place!' He laughs, as if he's delivering a funny monologue on some TV entertainment show. 'Why on earth would anybody do that? I'd be out of that house as fast as I possibly could! I'd make damned sure I was never alone with that person again. Mad!'

When the police asked Jonathan why all these boys – who have never met or even spoken to each other – had almost identical stories to tell, he replied that he didn't know. I am determined to ask at least one victim why he continually went back for more.

The defence argues that the police actively encouraged claims of emotional scarring when they interviewed the victims, because, without it, what else was there? Just some sex, long ago. The danger, says the defence team, is that if Jonathan is found guilty, the judge will sentence him not only for the acts themselves, but also for the quantity of emotional scarring the victims claim to have. And how can that be quantified, especially in this age of the self, when the whole world seems to be forever looking to their childhoods for clues as to why they turned out so badly?

'Jonathan King,' says David Jeremy, the prosecution barrister, in his opening remarks to the jury, 'was exploiting the young by his celebrity.'

When I first heard about King's arrest, I looked back at his press interviews for clues, and found a quote he gave *Music Week* magazine in 1997: 'I am a 15-year-old trapped inside a 52-year-old body.'

I talked to some of his friends from the pop industry, and one of them said, 'Poor Jonathan. We were all doing that sort of thing back then.'

I attended an early hearing at Staines Magistrates' Court. Jonathan King arrived in a chauffeured car. The windows were blacked out. Two builders watched him from a distance. As he walked past them and into the court, one of them yelled, 'Fucking nonce!'

He kept walking. Inside, he noticed me on the press benches. We had appeared together on Talk Radio a few years ago and he recognized me. On his way out, he gave me a lavish bow, as if I had just witnessed a theatrical event, starring him. Outside, the builders were still there. They shouted 'Fucking nonce!' again.

My email correspondence with Jonathan began soon after this hearing. In one email, he asked me if I would consider it fair if, say, Mick Jagger was arrested today for having sex with a fifteen-year-old girl in 1970. I agreed that it wouldn't be. He told me that he was being charged with the same crime that destroyed Oscar Wilde – the buggering of teenage boys – and we perceive Wilde to have been unjustly treated by a puritanical society from long ago. I wonder if the reason why we look less kindly upon Jonathan King is because he sang 'Jump Up and Down and Wave Your Knickers In the Air', while Oscar Wilde wrote *De Profundis*.

In another email, he wrote about Neil and Christine Hamilton, falsely accused of rape while being filmed by Louis Theroux, whom Jonathan sees as my great competitor in the humorous journalism market. He wrote, 'Louis EVERYWHERE . . . but who on earth would want to cover the Hamiltons, famous for doing NOTHING. Still, I do hope The Real Jon Ronson will have the balls, courage and integrity to take up the crusade (whatever the outcome) that it is GROSSLY unfair for the accused person/people to be smeared all over the media. Over to you, Ronson (we don't just want a Theroux treatment, do we?)'

Later, in court, some of the victims say that Jonathan had a trick of making them feel special, as if they could do anything, as if they could make it big in show business, just so long as they stuck with him (and didn't tell anyone what had happened). Has King got legitimate grievances against the legal system, or is he simply trying to seduce me in the same way he seduced the boys?

His Jagger analogy, I presume, was alluding to some covert homophobia at the heart of the case. But perhaps the real contrast lies somewhere else. Mick Jagger (or, indeed, Bill Wyman) wouldn't have needed to pretend he was conducting market research into the tastes of young people. He wouldn't have needed to have promised them sex with Colombian air hostesses. But Jonathan did not, intrinsically, have much pulling power, so he did need those extra little touches. Perhaps the real contrast, then, is one of aesthetics.

The Walton Hop closed down in 1990. There were complaints of noise from the neighbours. But the Hop's home, the Walton Playhouse, still stands. Jimmy Pursey, the lead singer of Sham 69, was one of the Hop's most regular teenage attendees. He went dancing there every

Tuesday, Friday and Saturday night throughout the seventies. One day, shortly before the trial began, Jimmy gave me a guided tour of the Playhouse.

'It's so hard to explain to people who see in black and white the colour that existed in this club,' he said. 'The Playhouse was a theatre for fringe plays and amateur dramatics. But on Tuesdays, Fridays and Saturdays it would become paradise.'

Jimmy took me through the hall, and towards the stage.

'It was inspirational,' said Jimmy. 'This wasn't table tennis. This was dancing. This was testing out your own sexuality. Normal people would become very unnormal. It was Welcome to the Pleasure Dome. It was everything.'

He leapt up onto the stage, and took me to the wings, stage right. We stood behind the curtains.

'This is where the inner sanctum was,' said Jimmy. 'From here, Deniz Corday would have the best view of the teenagers who were a little bit bolder, a little bit more interesting.'

'Bolder and interesting in what way?' I asked.

'People like me,' said Jimmy. 'If Deniz liked you, you'd be invited backstage and get a little bit of whisky added to your Coca-Cola. Backstage, you see. And you'd go, "Oh, I'm in with the big crowd now." That's all there was to it with Deniz.'

'And Jonathan?' I asked.

'He'd drive into the Hop car park, and come back-stage from the side,' he said. 'And we'd all be going, "God! There's a Rolls-Royce outside with a TV aerial coming from it! Ooh, it's got a TV in the back and it's a white Rolls-Royce!" Because you'd never know if it was the Beatles.'

'But it wasn't the Beatles,' I said.

'No,' said Jimmy. 'It was Jonathan King.' He laughed. 'A very big difference there!'

The Beatles lived on St George's Hill, in nearby Wey-bridge, and were often seen driving around Walton in their Rolls-Royces. The Walton area, in the seventies, was London's playpen, full of pop moguls and pop stars, letting their hair down, doing just what Jimmy said the teenagers at the Walton Hop did – being 'unnormal'.

In fact, a disproportionate number of celebrities who are now convicted paedophiles hung around backstage at the Walton Hop, this popular youth club, during the seventies and eighties. There was Jonathan King's friend Tam Paton, for instance, the manager of the Bay City Rollers, who was convicted of child-sex offences in the early eighties. (It was Paton who first introduced Jonathan King to the Hop – they met when Jonathan was invited to produce the Rollers' debut single, 'Keep On Dancing'.)

Chris Denning, the former Radio 1 DJ, was another Hop regular – he has a string of child-sex convictions, is currently in jail in Prague and was friendly with King and Paton.

For Jimmy Pursey, the trick was to pick up the girls who were drawn to the Hop to see the Bay City Rollers, while avoiding the attentions of the impresarios who orchestrated the night.

'It was fun with Deniz Corday,' said Jimmy. 'Deniz would say, "Oh, Jimmy! Come here! I'd love to suck your fucking cock!" Deniz was a silly, fluffy man. Then there was Tam Paton. I remember being back here having one of my whisky and Coca-Colas one night, and Tam turned to me and he said, "I like fucking lorry drivers." Chris Denning was more reckless. One time he placed his penis within the pages of a gay centrefold and showed it to my ex-bass player, who proceeded to kick the magazine, and Denning's dick, and yell, "Come on, Jimmy, we're fucking out of here!" But Jonathan King was more like a Victorian doctor. It wasn't an eerie vibe . . . but Jonathan had this highbrow, Cambridge, sophisticated thing about him. The Jekyll and Hyde thing. There wasn't much conversation with Jonathan. And with Jonathan, you'd always had these rumours. "Oh, he got so and so into the white Rolls-Royce." And they'd always be the David Cassidy lookalike-competition winners. Very beautiful.'

'Would he make a grand entrance?' I asked.

'Oh no,' said Jimmy. 'It was never, "Look at me!" He never went out onto the dance floor at all. He was much happier hiding backstage up here, behind the curtains, in the inner sanctum.' Jimmy paused. 'The same way he hid behind all those pseudonyms, see? He's always hiding. I think that's the whole thing of his life. He always says, "That was me behind Genesis! That was me behind 10cc! That was me behind all those pseudonyms." But what do you do then, Jonathan? Who are you then, Jonathan?'

Jimmy was referring to the countless pseudonymous novelty hits Jonathan had in the late sixties and seventies – The Piglets' 'Johnny Reggae', for instance, and Shag's 'Loop Di Love'. These came after his hugely successful 1965 debut, 'Everyone's Gone to the Moon', which was recorded while he was still a student at Cambridge. (Before that, he was a pupil at Charterhouse.) It was a remarkable career path: a lovely, plaintive debut, followed by a string of silly, deliberately irritating hits.

One of King's friends later suggests to me that it was his look – the big nose, the glasses, the weird lopsided grin – that determined this career path, as if he somehow came to realize that it was his aesthetic destiny to play the clown. But one cannot categorize his career as a downward spiral from 'Everyone's Gone to the Moon' onwards. In fact, he has sold forty million records. He's had a hand in almost every musical movement since the mid-sixties – psychedelic, novelty bubblegum pop, alternative pop, Eurovision, the Bay City Rollers, 10cc, *The Rocky Horror Show*, Genesis, Carter The Unstoppable Sex Machine, the Brit Awards and so on.

Within two years of leaving Cambridge, he was running Decca Records for Sir Edward Lewis, with his own West End offices and a Rolls-Royce parked outside.

'Genesis,' he once said, 'would have become accountants and lawyers if I hadn't heard their concealed and budding musical talent when they were fifteen years old.'

He is at once seen to be the quintessential Broadway Danny Rose – the buffoonish loser who was forever nearly making it – and also a powerful multimillionaire whose influence is as incalculable as it is overlooked. He's hosted radio shows in New York and London, presented the successful and long-running *Entertainment USA* TV series for the BBC, written two novels, created a political party – the Royalists – and published *The Tip Sheet*, an influential online industry magazine that, he claims, is responsible for bringing the Spice Girls, Oasis, Blur, Prodigy, R. Kelly, and others 'exploding on to musical success. We find and help break new stars around the world.'

In 1997, he was honoured with a lifetime achievement award by the Music Industry Trust. In a letter read out at the ceremony, Tony Blair acknowledged King's 'important contribution to one of this country's great success stories'.

A galaxy of stars – Peter Gabriel, Ozzy Osbourne, Simon Bates – came out to praise him, although no galaxy of stars is willing to do the same now that he's been accused of paedophilia.

Nonetheless, he seems to delight in being the man we love to hate (theatrically speaking: he is mortified when he thinks his arresting officers really do hate him).

'I love to infuriate,' Jonathan told me over coffee in his office, shortly before the trial began. 'I deliberately set out to irritate.'

'Of course,' I said, 'should you be convicted, people will hate you in a very different way. This is not a good climate in which to be accused of paedophilia.'

'Well,' he shrugged, 'it's not as though I'm sitting here thinking, "Oh, I'm such a nice person. Will everybody please be nice to me." I know I tend to provoke extreme reactions, so I'm not at all surprised when they arrive.'

There was a short silence.

'So you see what's happening now as a *continuation* of your public image?' I asked him.

'Absolutely,' said Jonathan. 'And it is so. And it would be absurd not to regard it as so.'

'But there's a difference between bringing out a novelty record that nobody likes and being accused of buggering an underage boy,' I said.

There was another silence. 'Let's not discuss it further,' he said.

11 September, day two of the trial, and things are already looking hopeless for him. The first victim – now a painter and decorator from the suburbs of North London – takes the stand. I'll call him David. Jonathan approached David in Leicester Square when David was fourteen or fifteen. Although David had no idea who Jonathan was, he quickly told him he was famous.

'It was exciting,' says David.

Jonathan gave David the questionnaire, the one that ranked boys' hobbies in order of preference. He filled it out. Jonathan invited him back to his house and asked him if he and his friends masturbated together. Jonathan showed him pornographic movies on a cine projector.

'We were talking about masturbation,' says David. 'He told me to relax. He undid my trousers. He tried to masturbate me, which didn't arouse me at all. He told me to do it myself, which I proceeded to do. I felt very awkward.'

David returned to King's house on three occasions. Similar indecent assaults occurred each time. Later, Jonathan wrote David a series of letters.

'He made it sound like I would be famous,' says David.

The prosecuting barrister asks David to read one of these letters to the jury.

' "Maybe you will go on to be a megastar. Now I am in New York. I will call you when I next hit town. In the meantime, keep tuning in on Wednesday at 9pm for *Entertainment USA*, the greatest TV show in the world." '

David says that Jonathan King has emotionally scarred him for life. He says he cannot hold children. He says it makes him scared and uncomfortable to hold and play with his girlfriend's little boy.

After lunch, Ron Thwaites, Jonathan's defence barrister, begins his cross-examination of David. His tone is breathtakingly abrasive.

'We are going back sixteen years because you decided not to make the complaint until nine months ago,' he says. 'You're not asking for sympathy for that, are you?'

'I was the one that was assaulted,' David replies, shakily.

'Do you think it's easy for a man to be accused of a crime after twenty years,' says Thwaites. And then: 'Are you interested in money?'

'I am nervous up here,' says David. 'You are putting me under pressure. I was sexually assaulted by that man over there.'

'You must have been fairly grown up to go to London on your own,' says Ron Thwaites. 'You can't have been a boy in short trousers, mewling for your mother.'

And so on.

We are unaware that, during this cross-examination, New York and Washington DC are under attack.

That night, I receive an email from Jonathan: 'Makes whether or not I put my hand on a teenager's knee 15 years ago seem rather trivial, doesn't it? Are you dropping KING for the World Trade Centre? Boo hoo! What do you think of the jury? A lot of ethnic variation which, I think, is probably a good thing. Not Ron's best day, but not terminal! See you tomorrow. Love JK.'

A week later, Jonathan posts an extraordinary message on his website, kingofhits.com: 'Well, it's been a fascinating couple of weeks. Not many people are fortunate to discover first hand exactly what Oscar Wilde went through! This week is the crucial one for me – keep praying. And just one oblique thought . . . when you look at the teenagers from 15 years ago who grew up to be terrorists who killed thousands in America, wonder what changed them into mass murderers. Then wonder what turns other decent teenagers into mass liars.'

Of course, they didn't turn out to have been lying.

King's demeanour remains cheerful throughout our time together. 'I am living in clouds and happy flowers and love and beauty,' he tells me one day. 'And if I go to prison, I shall enjoy myself.'

Even on the one occasion that Jonathan all but confesses to me – 'I'm sure you've got skeletons in your own closet, Jon. "Honest, guv! I thought she was sixteen!" ' – he says it with a spirited laugh.

When the *Guardian*'s photographer takes Jonathan's portrait early one morning before a day in court, he is frustrated to report that during almost every shot Jonathan stuck his thumbs up – as if he was doing a Radio 1 publicity session – or grinned his famous, funny, lopsided grin into the camera. This was not the image anyone wanted. We were hoping for something more revealing, sadder, perhaps, or even something that said 'child sex', or 'guilty'. But Jonathan wouldn't oblige.

One day during the trial, I hear a story about Larry Parnes, Britain's first pop mogul. He discovered Tommy Steele and Marty Wilde. Like many of the great British impresarios back then, he based his business judgements on his sexual tastes.

'If I am attracted to Tommy Steele,' he would tell his associates, 'teenage girls will be, too.'

Parnes's West End flat was often full of teenage boys hoping to be chosen as his next stars. If he liked the look of them, he'd give them a clean white T-shirt. Once he'd had sex with them, he'd make them take off the white T-shirt and put on a black one.

Wham!'s manager Simon Napier-Bell – who was once invited by Parnes to put on a white T-shirt – has said that the great difference between the British and American pop industries is this: the American impresarios are traditionally driven by money, while their British counterparts were historically driven by gay sex, usually with younger boys – and that British pop was conceived as a canvas upon which older gay Svengalis could paint their sexual fantasies, knowing their tastes would be shared by the teenage girls who bought the records. I wonder if the pop impresarios who seduced young teenage boys at the Walton Hop saw themselves not as a paedophile ring, but as the continuance of a venerable tradition.

Deniz Corday is desperately worried that the Walton Hop, his life's work, is about to become famous for something terrible.

'Jonathan didn't want me to talk to you,' he says, 'but I must defend the Hop with all my life.'

Deniz is immensely proud of the Hop. There is Hop

memorabilia all over his flat, including a poster from a Weybridge Museum exhibition, 'The Happy Hop Years 1958–1990. An Exhibition About Britain's First Disco: The Walton Hop'.

'Every day, someone comes up to me in the supermarket,' says Deniz, 'and says, "Thank you, Deniz, for making my childhood special." Some say the Hop was the first disco in Great Britain. It was terribly influential. Oh dear . . .' Deniz sighs. 'This kind of thing can happen in any disco. The manager can't control everything.'

Deniz says that he knows it looks bad. Yes, an unusually large number of convicted celebrity paedophiles used to hang around backstage at the Walton Hop. But, he says, they weren't there to pick up boys. They were there to conduct market research.

'Tam Paton would play all the latest Roller acetates and say, "Clap for the one you like the best." Same as Jonathan and Chris Denning. It helped them in their work.'

Deniz turns out the lights and gets out the Super-8 films he shot over the years at his club. Here's the Hop in 1958. Billy Fury played there. The teenagers are all in suits, dancing the hokey-cokey.

'Suits!' laughs Deniz, sadly.

The years tumble by on the Super-8 films. Now it's the mid-seventies. Here's Jonathan at the turntables. He's playing disco records, announcing the raffle winners and grinning his lopsided grin into Deniz's Super-8 camera. He's wearing his famous multi-coloured Afro wig. Now, on the Super-8, two young girls are on stage at the Hop, miming to King's song 'Johnny Reggae'. 'These were the days before karaoke,' explains Deniz.

For a while, we watch the girls on the stage mime to 'Johnny Reggae'. It turns out that Jonathan wrote it about a boy called John he met at the Walton Hop who was locally famous for his reggae obsession. David Jeremy – the prosecutor at the Old Bailey – says that Jonathan's 'market research' was simply a ploy, his real motive being to engage the boys in conversations about sex. But I imagine that the two endeavours were, in Jonathan's mind, indistinguishable. I picture Jonathan in the shadows, backstage at the Hop, taking all he could from the teenagers he scrutinized – consuming their ideas, their energy, their tastes, and then everything else.

The Super-8s continue in Deniz's living room. Here's Jonathan again, in 1983, backstage at the Hop. He's put on weight. He doesn't know the camera is on him. He's holding court to a group of young boys and girls on a sofa. You can just make out little snippets of conversation over the noise of the disco. He chews on a toothpick, looks down at a piece of paper, turns to a boy and says, 'Whose phone number is this?'

He spots the camera. 'It's Deniz Corday!' he yells. 'Look who it is! Deniz Corday! Smile at the camera!' He lifts up his T-shirt and Deniz zooms in on his chest.

'In thirty-two years,' says Deniz, 'we never had one complaint about Jonathan and young boys, and suddenly, after thirty-two years, all these old men, grandfathers some of them, come forward and say they've been sexually abused and it's been bothering them all their lives. I think there's something deeply suspicious about it. Jonathan's a really nice guy and definitely not a paedophile. Anyway, I think it should be reworded. I think a paedophile should be someone who goes with someone under thirteen.'

The clothes and hairstyles change as the decades roll past on the Super-8s, but the faces of the thirteen-to-eighteen-year-olds remain the same. They are young and happy. Deniz says that, nowadays, we have an absurdly halcyon image of childhood. He says that the youngsters at the Walton Hop were not fragile little flowers. They were big and tough and they could look after themselves. He rifles through his drawer and produces some of the police evidence statements. He reads me some excerpts.

' "There was a crate of Coca-Cola kept backstage, and it was people like Jonathan King and Corday who hung around there. If you were invited back there you would get a free Coke with a shot of whisky." '

Deniz pauses. 'Now how ridiculous can you get? I'm going to give the kids of the Hop a shot of whisky with a Coke?'

There is a silence.

'Well,' he says quietly. 'If I gave them a little bit of whisky once in a while, they're not going to put me in jail for it. I used to call it "Coke with a kick". Anyway, we're not talking about me. We're talking about Jonathan. Have you heard of any charges against me?'

'No,' I say.

'Exactly,' says Deniz. 'This is about Jonathan. Not about me.'

Deniz continues to read. The victim making the statement describes life at the Walton Hop and how Jonathan – a regular visitor – once went out of his way to talk to him.

' "I was obviously excited to be talking to Jonathan King. He offered to give me a lift home, which I accepted. This was the first of many lifts King gave me, and I recall that he always drove me home in a white convertible Rolls-Royce. It was an automatic car and the number plate was JK9000. We talked about music, and he often told me that he needed a young person's point of view. King drove me home on a couple of occasions before he eventually assaulted me. The first assault occurred at a car park, which was situated on the left-hand side of the

Old Woking Road. Next to the car park was a field and a wooded area. King seemed familiar with the location. I believe he had been there before. I was sat in the front passenger seat and King was in the driver seat. I noticed that King had started shaking, and I presumed that he needed the toilet." '

Deniz laughs.

'Well, you can laugh occasionally,' he says.

He continues to read. ' "He then leant over to where I was sat. To my horror he started pulling at my trousers. He wrenched my trousers open and he just went for it." '

Deniz reads the statement with mock, burlesque horror.

' "He had his face in my lap and he was performing oral sex on me by putting his mouth around my penis. I was so shocked." '

Deniz looks up. 'He doesn't say if he had an erection!' he laughs.

' "After a while he stopped performing oral sex on me, and although my penis was erect I did not ejaculate. I then noticed that King had his trousers undone with his penis exposed and he started masturbating himself. I remember looking out of the window and contemplating walking home. I did not because I just hoped that once he was done he would drop me home. King eventually came and he then drove me home. I didn't want Jonathan to tell Deniz what had happened, because I thought he'd want to do the same thing."

'No thanks, mate,' says Deniz, before carrying on with the statement.

' "I felt sick and ashamed about what he had done to me, and I remember looking in the mirror the next day and wondering if you could see what had happened in my face. The second assault on me by King took place near the car park which had been previously described. This time he buggered me . . . Once at the location, we got out of the car and he then led me about fifteen yards to a dip in a wooded area. King led me by placing one hand on the back on my neck and the other on my arm. King was shaking. King then took my trousers and underwear down. He then forced his penis inside my anus and penetrated me. I would describe King as frantic at the time. He was totally uncaring. I honestly believe if I had said no, he would have forced me. King had his underwear and trousers down by his ankles and he used no lubrication. I can also say that he did not have a huge penis." '

Deniz laughs. 'I'm glad to hear that, mate!' he says.

' "Although he was rough, it was not painful. I was in a state of shock. King eventually came inside of me and it was all very quick. Not only did I wash that night, but

I constantly washed myself that week. I hated what he had done to me and I felt dirty. It may be that King grabbed some of my hair, because for about a week washed my hair everyday which was most unlike me. I even remember my dad making some comment about me using so much shampoo. The third time King assaulted me was . . ." '

Deniz looks up angrily. 'How many times do you have to go back before you decide that you don't like being fucked? Does it take three sexual experiences for you to realize it was bothering you? "The third time King assaulted me was, again, following a lift home from the Hop. This time it did hurt and I told him that, but he did not stop. I even asked him if he used Vaseline, and he replied, "Oh no, you'll do with spit." It all happened very fast, and he was very surgical and physical. I would also like to add that King never kissed me or showed me any affection. Many years later, I attended the Brit Awards, and while I was there I saw Jonathan King. On seeing me, he gave me a long stare and then walked away. I believe he is dangerous and I want to stop it happening to other children." '

Deniz looks up, in fury, from the evidence statement.

'He wasn't a child!' he says.

'How old was he?' I say.

'Fifteen,' says Deniz.

In the end, Jonathan is acquitted of this particular charge. The victim admits on the witness stand that he was probably sixteen when he knew Jonathan, and the prosecution can't prove that the sex was non-consensual. While there is no statute of limitations for underage sex – or for sexual assaults – a sixteen-year-old who has had consensual sex with an adult must, by law, complain within a year of the offence for the adult to be tried. This boy waited twenty-three years, which is why his case is abandoned.

The day after I see Deniz, I receive an email: 'Hope you'll remember Deniz is not quite as worldly wise as others – don't hurt him. JK.'

I always find it hard to look Jonathan in the eye after hearing some detailed recital of his sexual behaviour. But I wonder whether any act of sex, when described with such precision, would sound equally unpleasant. The evidence Deniz read me constitutes probably the most serious charge of all sixteen complaints, and even it is not as black and white as one might like. Why, for instance, did the victim return on two occasions?

I would like to ask Jonathan his views on the intricacies of these sexual power-plays, but he professes his innocence so adamantly that he won't be drawn on the subject. I do, however, get to ask another of his victims, Nick McMeier, these questions. One morning in November, I sit in Nick's flat in Kingston, Surrey, and he shows me some of the presents Jonathan bought him during their time together.

'Whenever I visited, I'd end up with two or three records,' says Nick. 'So I guess you can calculate how many times I visited him on that basis.'

I look at the pile of records. 'There must be thirty or forty records here,' I say. 'Or more.'

'And he gave a copy of his book *Bible 2*,' says Nick. 'And a guitar. And a biography of Edie Sedgwick.'

Jonathan also took Nick on trips – to the Walton Hop, for instance, and to Deniz's house, although nothing happened there. He gave him driving lessons in his TR7 in the car park of Chessington World of Adventure. 'It sounds like he thought that the two of you were having a relationship,' I say, 'that he wasn't your abuser, he was your boyfriend.'

'I don't know,' says Nick. 'He enjoyed being assertive. He was never particularly shy about name-dropping or describing just how famous he was.' Nick laughs. 'There was one occasion where we were in his Rolls-Royce in London and he pulled out in front of somebody and they beeped him and he turned round and said, "Do you mind? There's a famous person here!" And we carried on driving. It made me laugh at the time because it was true. He was a famous person.'

'Do you think that if you'd stopped being star-struck, he would have lost interest in you?' I ask.

'Yes,' says Nick.

Nick is thirty-four, and very good looking. He tells me how they first met. He was between fourteen and sixteen – he can't exactly remember – and he was cycling home from Richmond Park when Jonathan King pulled over in his Rolls-Royce and asked him directions to the Kingston bypass.

'I gave him the directions and then he said, "Do you know who I am?" Actually, no. He said, "You do realize who I am?" And I said, "Yeah. I do." I tried to act as un-star-struck as I possibly could.'

As they stood there on the road, Jonathan asked Nick to phone the BBC and tell them just how much he enjoyed his TV shows and could they please commission more from him. Nick agreed, although he never did phone.

They swapped phone numbers and Jonathan called several weeks later and invited him to his flat.

'We listened to some records, had a bit of a chat. He showed off his mirrored toilet. He said, "Take a look in there, it's pretty impressive." So I went in there and was duly impressed. And that was pretty much it.'

This was the only time that no sex took place. On every other occasion, Jonathan buggered Nick.

'Why did you keep going back?' I ask.

There is a silence.

'I don't really know. Well, I was getting records every time. But I was also enjoying the sexual gratification. I wasn't racked with guilt. At that age, you've got the hormones raging around inside you. And I felt taken care of. I knew that wasn't how grown-ups normally took care of children, but he had a kind of invincibility about him. A self-assurance.'

Nick's relationship with Jonathan King lasted eighteen months. In the intervening years, he has come to identify the extent of the emotional scarring those months caused him. He has just completed six weeks of therapy which, he says, has barely scratched the surface.

'It caused a division between my emotional side and myself,' he says. 'It was like I put my emotions in a room and shut the door. It's not even something I was aware of happening until I spoke to the police and they came to interview me. And two days later this incredible dark cloud came over me, like a black dog. It also bothers me quite a lot that I was lying to my parents. He even came round one Christmas and met the whole family. We got together a Christmas stocking for him with a pound coin in the bottom of it and a satsuma.'

Nick says that he has seen the message Jonathan posted on his website, comparing his victims to the terrorists who attacked the World Trade Centre.

'I think he's rather a sad, impotent man,' says Nick, 'whose chickens have come home to roost.' He laughs. 'But that's probably a coping mechanism for myself to disenfranchise him of any power.'

On day five of the trial, one of the victims says in court that Jonathan had a blue door, when in fact his door was white. This presumably trivial inaccuracy gives rise to the following email from Jonathan: 'The accusers have provenly lied on oath – blue front door etc. Will the CPS prosecute them for perjury? Rather doubt it. If the verdicts are guilty, they collect their cash from the Compensation Board . . . Is this right or fair? A topic you may feel inclined to raise in your wonderful story. See you later. JK'

And so on. Each time an email from Jonathan appears in my inbox, I open it with excitement, envisaging a startling insight into his character, or into the complex sexual relationships between older pop moguls and young boys, but usually they're full of these red herrings.

Most of the conversations that occur in the Old Bailey canteen between the journalists centre not on Jonathan King but on Ron Thwaites, his extraordinary, shocking, charismatic defence barrister.

'Ron could get the Devil off,' one veteran tabloid Old Bailey reporter tells me.

Before the trial even started, during the preparatory

hearings in July, Thwaites had great success in reducing the charges against his client. 'Lots of people,' he said to Judge Paget, 'don't enjoy sex.'

Lots of people don't enjoy sex – but this doesn't mean that assaults have been committed against them. Where's the guilty mind if the boys appeared to acquiesce? An assailant, he argued, must know he's committing an assault for a crime to have occurred. But there were no protestations. Nowhere in the evidence did a boy admit to saying 'No!' or 'Stop!' And if they really hated it – if it scarred them – why wait twenty years to come forward! Thirty years!

David Jeremy, the prosecution barrister, argued that the look on their faces would have suggested protestation.

Thwaites contended that if King was having anal sex with them, he wouldn't have seen the look on their faces.

Yes, said Thwaites, King approached boys. He approached thousands of boys.

'These encounters,' he said, 'are the tip of the iceberg.'

But he did not approach them for sex. He approached them for market research.

'My client interacts with his public,' he said, 'on a grand scale.'

I looked over at the arresting officers. They chuckled wryly at the words 'tip of the iceberg'.

Then Thwaites attacked the police, accusing them of underhand tactics. If a complainant said he was between fourteen and sixteen when the assault allegedly occurred, the police wrote that he was fourteen. He asked for six of the complainants to be struck off the charge sheet, and the judge agreed to four of them. Thwaites also asked for three trials instead of one, for the purposes of 'case management'.

The prosecution, startled by this suggestion, argued that this would harm their best evidence – the pattern of King's seduction. But, bafflingly, Judge Paget agreed to split the trials.

'Oh, fuck,' whispered an arresting officer, putting his head in his hands, when the judge announced his decision.

The unspoken assumption, shared by all parties, was that there would never be three trials. The prosecution was likely to throw in the towel after trials one or two, whatever the outcome. So the preparatory hearing turned out to be a great victory for King and Thwaites.

Every day, in the Old Bailey, Ron Thwaites launches another merciless attack on anybody he can think of who is not his client. The victims are 'cranks' who 'came out of the woodwork' seeking 'compensation'. This includes one who cried in the witness box. 'Crocodile tears!' he snarls. Others are 'drug addicts and fantasists and liars'. One is 'completely mad'.

Admittedly, Thwaites does have something of a point here. One of the victims, Chris Sealey, admits within five minutes of cross-examination that he sees black cats that nobody else can see and thinks that gypsies are going to come to his house to rip out his throat. Chris also admits that he came forward solely for the money. He hopes to sell his story to a newspaper. (He does: to the *Sunday People*, embellishing his testimony with extraordinary relish.)

Chris's argument is, 'So what?' Jonathan King got something out of him, so why shouldn't he get something out of Jonathan King?

Thwaites even brings me into the mix at one point. During his summing up he points in my direction and says to the jury, 'I cannot prove that there is a contract in which [the complainants] have agreed to appear on TV or in the newspapers . . .'

His implication seems to be that the Ronson–Victim financial pact is so cunning that the poor, justice-seeking defence team cannot break through its steely ramparts. The real reason why Thwaites cannot prove this contract exists is, of course, because it doesn't (Nick does not want to be paid for our interview), but I cannot let the jury know this. I just have to sit there. From a distance, the game-playing between prosecution and defence in an Old Bailey trial might seem gallant, but close up I sometimes find it quite horrible.

But Thwaites does highlight some of the unfortunate aspects of the case. There is no material evidence. No DNA. How can King defend himself against crimes that occurred so long ago?

'Justice delayed,' says Thwaites, 'is justice denied.'

Nonetheless, for all of Thwaites' mini-victories, Jonathan tells me he has already packed his bags, all ready for a guilty verdict. He says he has brought every book on the Booker Prize shortlist in preparation for life in jail.

On day 10 of the trial, a defence strategy backfires alarmingly. After days of prosecution evidence outlining the nefarious ways in which Jonathan would make a frantic show of his celebrity status to awe his victims into acquiescence, Thwaites plays for the jury a videotape of the highlights of Jonathan King's career.

In the video, Jonathan is seen hosting the 1987 Brit Awards and receiving the 1997 Man of the Year Award. There are shots of him on *Top of the Pops* singing 'Una Paloma Blanca' and 'Everyone's Gone to the Moon'. I have no idea why Jonathan thinks it might be a good idea to show this in court. He is clearly trying to awe the jury in the same way that he awed the boys. I presume that there is no grand scheme behind this tactic, and that Jonathan simply wants to show off.

It takes the jury three days to reach a verdict. The night before they finally do, Jonathan sends me an email that reads: 'Pray for me.'

I don't email him back. I have grown to like Jonathan King, but he is guilty. As likeable as he is, he did it. Perhaps there is some homophobia in this case. Bill Wyman, after all, got away with having sex with a younger girl. Is it unfair, as Jonathan claims, that his initial high-profile arrest was simply a way for the police to advertise for more victims to come forward? Most observers agree that the prosecution would never have secured a conviction with the initial complainants' allegations, and that the police were hoping for more reliable witnesses to come forward. Is it unfair, or clever police-work?

I don't see Jonathan in the canteen or the lobby on the day of the verdict, but I do see him in the dock, as the jury files in. He smiles at me. Every male juror makes a point of looking at Jonathan as they take their seats. The women all look away. The clerk of the court asks the foreman for the verdict on the first count, and he says, 'Guilty.'

Jonathan nods.

Then it is time for count two – the most serious charge. Buggery. This is the charge that relates to Chris Sealey. The foreman says, 'Guilty.'

Jonathan nods.

There are six guilty verdicts in total. A clean sweep. Judge Paget says that, under these circumstances, bail must be revoked. Within seconds, Jonathan is led downstairs from the dock, and straight to Belmarsh Prison.

The blood drains from his face as he is taken down. In the very last second, as he is led through the door – the last time I see him – he buckles and nearly falls.

Little Kellerstain, Tam Paton's large, outlandish, rural bungalow near Edinburgh airport, his home for twenty-seven years, give or take his twelve months in jail for child-sex offences and the years travelling the world in Lear jets and limousines with his young charges, the Bay City Rollers, is noisy today. You imagine it to have always been a noisy place. Indeed, the old neighbours, the now dead rich couple who lived next door at the grand Kellerstain House, used to complain bitterly about their eccentric, legendary, pop-impresario neighbour, the packs of screaming Roller fans forever camped outside his electric gates, the parties, the teams of police officers searching his house for clues of paedophile activity and then more screaming – the screams of the headlines:

'Sordid Secrets of Twisted Tam', 'Tam's Night in the Sauna with the Boys'.

Today, the place is noisy with dogs and boys. The dogs are Rottweilers. There are four of them, and they seem to hate each other. There are about half a dozen boys living with Tam. They live in spare rooms and in caravans in the garden. They are all around eighteen years old. Tam is sixty-three now. He is polite to a fault, almost humble. It is as if the years of being considered a paedophile, a pervert, have reduced him to a position of constant subservience around strangers. The Tam Paton of today is nothing like the fearsome Svengali you would see on television during the Roller years.

I have come to see Paton because of the similarities in his and Jonathan King's crimes. They were friends and colleagues, and would visit the Hop together. Like Jonathan, the boys Paton 'indecently assaulted' were not that young. The youngest was fifteen. I know that it will take Jonathan years to settle into his new role in life as a convicted celebrity paedophile. Paton has had twenty years to do this. So I imagine that meeting him will be like meeting Jonathan in the future.

'I was jailed for six years for underage sex,' says Tam. 'Underage sex. Under the age of twenty-one. This was 1981. I served a year. My victims were ... one was fifteen. I never even touched him. There was nothing physical in that particular charge. The chap was deaf and he had a speech impediment. He came to my house and he saw a pornographic movie, a heterosexual pornographic movie.'

'What was it called?' I ask.

'*Tina with the Big Tits*,' says Tam. 'This happened right here in this very room. It was all to do with women's boobs. Big boobs. All sizes of boobs. And he'd had two lagers. The charges that were raised against me was that I'd subjected a fifteen-year-old handicapped boy to pornographic movies and supplied him with stupefying alcohol with intent to pervert and corrupt. I got six months right there for that.'

Tam takes me to the scene of more of his crimes – his sauna room. It was built in the seventies, in what used to be his utility room. He turns on the Jacuzzi. It bubbles into life. 'I got six months for putting my hand on a guy's leg in the sauna,' says Tam. 'And then I got another two years for a chap who willingly came up here. He was sixteen, educated, a nice guy. He came up in a taxi. I gave him a bottle of Lambrusco.'

Of course, the stigma of being imprisoned for underage-sex crimes remains with Tam to this day. Just last week, one of his friends – who has a three-month-old baby – was visited by social services and warned that the baby should be kept away from Tam Paton.

'A tiny little baby!' says Tam. 'People look at me like I'm an animal. People who don't know me judge me. I always remember going up to visit someone in prison, and this woman was sitting there. She was looking at me, growling a bit, and I could imagine what she was thinking: "There's a paedophile!" Anyway, I later discovered about her character. And I'll tell you, it outweighed anything I'd ever done.'

'What had she done?' I asked.

'Shoplifting,' says Tam.

There is a silence.

'People have their own little guilt trips,' says Tam. 'They look around. "Who's a beast? Who's a paedo?" Now it's on my record for the rest of my life. If I want to go into business, I have to state that I was done for lewd and libidinous. Gross indecency. People think, "Oh my God! He must have been crawling about in a nursery."'

'Can I ask about the boys who live here?' I say. 'What do they do?'

'They clean up,' he replies, a little sharply. 'They feed the dogs. They take them for walks. They help me with my property business. They are eighteen years of age, and I don't have a relationship with them. You can interview them until the cows come home. Maybe I just like nice people floating about. We don't have orgies. There's no swinging from the chandeliers. Even if there was,' he adds, 'it would be legal.'

Tam believes he was targeted because of his fame, because he was a celebrity Svengali. He blames his arrest, then, on the pop business. And now he is out of it. He has become a property millionaire, with forty flats in Edinburgh's West End.

'I do get myself upset,' he says. 'I've given away all the Roller albums to charity. I want to forget it all. I've had two heart attacks. And now the same thing is happening with Jonathan. A fox hunt. Everyone wants to see the death of the fox. They would never have gone after us if we were heterosexual. But if you're a poof, my God.'

I change the subject.

'Do you think you have emotionally scarred any of the boys for life?' I ask.

Tam looks startled – as if he's never considered this possibility before. 'Oh my God,' he says. 'I hope not.'

In mid-October 2001, I have coffee with Jonathan King's brother, Andy. He's just visited Jonathan in Belmarsh for the first time.

'How is Jonathan doing?' I ask.

'Great,' says Andy. 'He seems really cheerful. Talking ten to a dozen.'

'Really?' I ask.

'He's wearing pink pyjamas as a silent protest,' Andy tells me. 'He says it's aesthetically reminiscent of the way gays were treated under the Nazis.'

On 20 November, things take a turn for the better for Jonathan. He is acquitted of buggery and indecent assault in the second trial – the witness admits on the stand that he was sixteen and not fifteen. The Crown Prosecution Service announces that same day that it won't proceed with any more trials – this includes the allegations from boys who said Jonathan King had picked them up at the Walton Hop.

The next morning, Jonathan is sentenced to seven years. Judge Paget says that the case is a tragedy. This otherwise honourable man, he says, this successful celebrity, used and abused his fame and success to attract impressionable teenagers. But there was no violence, no threats used.

Jonathan smiles and nods as he is sentenced. One journalist says that he looks smug; another says that he looks pale and beaten. His name is placed indefinitely on the sex offenders' list. The police say he may have abused hundreds of boys over the past thirty years. King's defence team say that they will now consider appealing.

Postscript

Jonathan King wrote to me throughout his prison sentence, and sent me Christmas cards, etc. For a while I was getting Christmas cards from Jonathan, and messages from the equally incarcerated Jeffrey Archer. I felt like one of those women. Jonathan continued to profess his innocence, although I never knew whether he meant it literally or metaphorically. He certainly did it. I wrote back once or twice, but that was all.

He was convicted of one buggery and five or six lesser offences. After the trial was over I asked Jonathan's solicitor why they didn't plead guilty to the lesser charges and fight the buggery one. (Personally I think Jonathan was guilty on all counts.) If they'd done that he probably would have got no more than a year or two.

He replied, 'You try defending His Nibs.'

I wasn't the only journalist Jonathan wrote to from prison. The *Observer*'s Lynn Barber published a brilliant article about their pen-pal friendship. Her husband David Cardiff (who was my teacher at college) was dying, and Jonathan had proved to be a 'wonderful confidant', she wrote. She visited him at Maidstone Prison and reported that he was walking around wearing a T-shirt that read, 'I'm a celebrity – get me out of here!'

'The very qualities – the relentless cheeriness, bump-tiousness and optimism – which made him seem quite irritating on the outside seem absolutely heroic in prison,' she wrote.

Just before Christmas 2001, a few weeks after the *Guardian* published my story about the case, I had a telephone call from the former Radio 1 DJ Chris Den-ning. Back in the seventies, Denning and Jonathan were best friends and business partners. Denning had, days earlier, been released from a three-year jail sentence in Prague for child-sex offences. The night before his depor-tation from the Czech Republic, I met him at a down-at-heel hotel off Wenceslas Square. He wouldn't say which country he was going to. (It turned out to be Austria.) He faced a number of similar offences in Britain, and he told me he'd be arrested if he ever returned here.

He turned up with a boy. He introduced him as one of the boys he'd just been in prison for, and he said he brought him along to prove they were still friends. The boy had flu, and throughout the interview he sat on the bed, sniffing, and looking bored and ill.

I asked Chris Denning if Jonathan King had learned how to pick up boys from him.

'That's possible,' he said. 'He did steal some of the things I did.'

'Like what?' I asked.

'I would make funny remarks,' he said. 'I'd be walking down the street with a couple of my younger friends and I'd say something absolutely absurd to a passer-by. I remember one joke I had. I'd say to a passer-by, "Excuse me, do you know where so and so street is?" And they'd say, "No. I'm sorry, I don't." And I'd say, "Oh, I can help you! It's just down there on the left . . .!" And for young people – for somebody like me to make a joke like that, it was hilarious.'

Chris Denning – despite his various jail sentences and the fact that he'd been sleeping rough in a Prague cemetery for the past week, on and off – still had the looks and voice and demeanour of an old-style Smashy and Nicey type of Radio 1 DJ.

'But Jonathan's humour always had a streak of cruelty,' Denning added, 'and I've always tried not to do that. I hate that kind of thing. Once I was going along in his car to Brighton. He'd invited a couple of young people I knew. He'd said, "Why don't you bring them along for the trip?" He had a chauffeur. He said, "James! To Brighton!" I was sitting in the Rolls-Royce with my shoes half off and he grabbed them and chucked them out of the window. I said to the chauffeur, "James. Can you please stop? I want to get my shoes." Jonathan said to him, "If you stop, you're fired. Drive on."'

'What did the boys in the car think of it?' I asked.

'I don't think they liked it,' he said. 'It was funny, you see, but it was cruel.'

We got onto the subject of whether I'd been unfair to Jonathan in my story. I said the thing that swayed me was that all twenty-seven men who came forward said they had been emotionally damaged.

Chris Denning sighed. 'Well, they *have* to say that,' he said.

'There is *no way* that twenty-seven men were doing it for the compensation,' I said.

'OK,' he said.

He paused.

'Maybe they *are* damaged,' he said. 'But there is no way of knowing – proving – that it had anything to do with one particular origin.'

'But they *all* say they were damaged,' I said.

'There's no reason why they *should* be damaged as long as it is consensual,' he said. 'Why? What difference does it make between sixteen and fifteen and a half, or fourteen? It's so easy to just excuse your failures in life. "Oh, that was the cause of it." It's a *guess*.'

Lots of Jonathan's friends had said this same thing to me. Many newspaper commentators had also raised this point in columns and editorials at the time of his conviction. Carol Sarler wrote in the *Observer*, 'The man they call Victim Two set much of the scene for the rest with his heart-tugging description of the disaster that his life has become: a rotten lousy mess of drugs and alcohol and crime – and all because he met Jonathan King! [Did the jury] really believe he might otherwise have been Einstein? . . . One gave evidence to the effect that he had not greatly enjoyed the sex, but that King gave him £40 – about two weeks' wages then – and he had gone back the following week for more; well sorry, M'Lud, but in the real world that's called trade. Consensual, low-rent trade.'

In the hotel room in Prague, Chris Denning asked me if I wanted to know the worst thing about being attracted to underage boys.

'Sadly,' he said, 'they grow up. They disappear. The person you were attracted to has gone. He doesn't exist anymore. You can never have a lasting relationship with them. It's very sad.'

In August 2005, Chris Denning returned to London from Austria. He was arrested at Heathrow Airport, and in February 2006 was convicted of child-sex offences, dating back to the seventies and eighties. He was sentenced to four years in prison. That same week, I received the following email:

Dear Jon,
I was abused by King's mate Chris Denning
who, as you know, has just been banged up.

*I recently sent this email to King. You may find it
amusing.*

Dear Jonathan,
*I see your old mate Chris Denning has been given
another serve of porridge. Hardly seems fair that
he only got four years and you got seven, but then
again you are an extremely repulsive and smarmy
cunt and one can't really blame the judge for
wanting to shaft you.*

*You are no doubt aware that your ex employer
the Sun has published a piece linking you to
Denning as members of a 'paedophile ring'. May
I make a suggestion Jonathan, this could be a
blessing in disguise, an opportunity to restore
your tattered reputation. Why don't you sue the
Sun Jonathan? How dare they link you to that vile
pervert Denning! After all you are a wronged
man, a 'victim' of your own celebrity. A modern
day Oscar Wilde. And after all it's not your fault
that twelve year old boys are so damn sexy, and
of course they all wanted it, why wouldn't an
adolescent boy want to be pawed and fucked up
the arse by a slavering, fat, ugly pig like your
good self. I expect they were beating down your
door Jonathan, how unfair that you should be*

*persecuted for providing these boys with a
'service'. Such a cruel world.*

*My dear sweet Jonathan I am not sure what
lies beyond the great divide, I try to live a good
life and I hope to die with honour. I am however
sure of one thing. That is this. When you die you
will be met by them and welcomed, the suicides,
and the ones who chose to die slowly by bottle
and by needle. And they shall take you in their
arms dear Jonathan, and embrace you for all
eternity.*

Your friend,
Simon

8. BLOOD SACRIFICE

On a Friday afternoon in January 2002, Susan Ellis sneaks past the security staff at Guy's Hospital, London. She's pretending to be a patient, although nobody asks. She catches the lift to the fourth floor, finds the kidney-dialysis waiting room, and whispers to me, 'It's perfect.'

And, for her purposes, it is. It's easily accessible from the corridor and security is not tight. It's almost empty of patients and staff. Most crucially, there's a table full of magazines. Susan pretends to read them. Nobody notices as she slips business cards inside the pages. She hopes patients will leaf through the magazines and see her card, which reads: 'Need a kidney transplant? I can donate a kidney to you for free. Contact me at: kidney_for_free_from_me@yahoo.co.uk. This is a genuine free offer.'

Donating kidneys to strangers is illegal in the UK. When I called the Department of Health to ask why, they said, 'You mean, strangers selling kidneys?'

'No. Just giving them away.'

There was a silence: 'Giving them away?'

'Yes.'

'You mean, when the donor is dead?'

'No, alive.'

'We'll get back to you,' they said. They did, with a prepared statement: 'Ultra [the Unrelated Live Transplant Regulatory Authority] insists on confirmation of an emotional relationship between a donor and a recipient.'

The DoH's view, they explained over the phone, is that anyone who wants to donate a kidney to a stranger must be in it for money. If they're not, they must have psychiatric problems, and so they need to be protected from themselves. No one would go through such a traumatic, invasive operation for sane, altruistic reasons. When I met Ultra's chairman, Sir Roddy McSween, he said he was sympathetic to altruistic donors in general, but added that the law's the law, and any infringement would result in three months in prison and a £2,000 fine.

Susan already knows about the illegality of strangers donating to strangers, so her plan is this: once a recipient contacts her, they will together concoct a story about how they've been best friends for years. They will prove this long-standing friendship with faked photographs. Some of Susan's wedding photos, she says, could easily be doctored – a recipient's head superimposed onto a bridesmaid's body, etc. If this plan fails, Susan will try to donate abroad.

Susan is a Jesus Christian. She has long forsaken her possessions to live in a camper van currently parked next to a jogging track in Catford, South-east London. Even though the Jesus Christians have been widely labelled as a sinister cult by the media and anti-cult groups, there is nothing externally odd about them – no unusual rituals, or anything like that. They simply spend their days keeping fit, discussing theological matters, and hanging around shopping precincts handing out cartoon books that look like Simpsons comics but, in fact, depict, among other parables, the persecution of the Jesus Christians by the courts, the media and the anti-cult groups.

The lifestyle is the thing. The Jesus Christians alone, they believe, are obedient to the teachings of Jesus, particularly Luke 14:33: 'Whosoever he be of you that forsaketh not all that he hath, he cannot be my disciple.' They have forsaken everything: families, possessions, jobs, homes, their place in the outside world, and are now in the process of giving up their spare kidneys, too, en masse.

A year ago, their leader Dave McKay was flying home to Australia after visiting his followers in the UK, India and the US. The in-flight entertainment was *Transplants: A Gift of Life*, a TV movie about a boy who donates his kidney to his grandmother. Dave was profoundly moved, and that's when he had the idea. In a round robin to his followers (there are around two dozen Jesus Christians worldwide; Dave's strict lifestyle criteria tend to keep the numbers down), he emailed his own intention to donate a kidney to a stranger. He also wrote, 'If anyone else is interested in doing the same, let me know.' The majority took him up on the offer.

Dave imagines that when the world learns of his mass kidney-donating plan, we'll regard it in one of two ways – either as a really lovely thing for the Jesus Christians to do, or as the self-destructive act of a religious cult acting under the spell of a notorious leader. I am surprised to learn later that he is not only expecting the latter response, he is hoping for it.

Susan has been researching and strategizing. As well as the business cards, she's been posting messages in chat rooms where people with failing kidneys support each other emotionally while they queue, often in vain, for a transplant. At an Internet cafe in Sutton, she checks her account to see if anyone has responded to her latest messages. There are scores of emails for her. The first is from the chat-room host: 'I do not wish to be associated with anything that could be construed as illicit as this would risk the group being shut down. I will discuss this matter with my son who's a police chief inspector and get back to you.'

Susan laughs nervously. 'Whoah!' she says.

She clicks on to the next email, which reads: 'You are probably using this opportunity to get into the USA. Sorry, but no black-market organs here. Stay in your own country.'

'Why is everyone taking this the wrong way?' sighs Susan.

She clicks on to the next email, from Portsmouth: 'What are you? Some kind of sick moron? This is no fun. Don't mess around with us. We have a severe illness. Can't imagine anyone would donate a kidney to a stranger without any strings.'

And then the next one: 'You're sick. How can you give people false hope like that? A lot of these people are on dialysis, waiting for a kidney, and Mrs Christianity has got two good ones! Whoopee for you! What are you going to do? Eenie, meeny, minie, mo, or a raffle? You're one sick attention-seeker. If you're for real, why be so desperate to send so many ads? You sound sad, lonely and unwanted. The gate you'll be touching when your number is up is bound to be hot.'

There is a silence.

'Hasn't he got a point?' I ask.

She looks hurt. 'Not the going to hell,' I clarify, 'but the . . .'

'The eenie, meeny, minie, mo?' says Susan. 'Sure. But that's like *Schindler's List*, right? He had an eenie, meeny, minie, mo situation, too, but what was he supposed to do – nothing? Just because there's a greater need than what you can give, doesn't mean you shouldn't give.'

And then she clicks on to the next email: 'Hi, I just received your email about you giving away one of your kidneys for free. I'm curious why you would want to do such a thing, and for NOTHING? I'm sorry, but I find it hard to believe. I don't want to be rude but I'm 36 years old and I had a kidney transplant – my third – about five years ago, and have been told it's failing and will be needing dialysis shortly. I'm not looking to get your kidney. I'm just interested in hearing your reasons. Sincerely, C.'

Susan is thrilled. 'I'm jumping up and down. I'm so happy.' She says she'll write back to C, who lives in Scotland, and perhaps strike up a friendship with her.

And then Susan returns to her camper van and her eight-year-old son, Danny, who is unaware that his mother wants to donate one of her kidneys to a stranger. Whenever I'm in their van, and we're talking about kidneys, and Danny runs in to ask his mother a question, we have to stop talking abruptly.

At the same time, in the US – where altruistic kidney donors are welcomed at a handful of hospitals – two Jesus Christians are ready to donate, in Minneapolis, on 21 February. Robin is thirty-six and has been a Jesus Christian for twenty-one years. Casey is twenty-three, and joined the group only in 2001. Like Susan, they decided to donate after Dave sent his email. I telephone Casey in early February, three weeks before his scheduled operation. 'Have you told your mother?' I ask him.

'No,' he says.

'Why not?' I ask.

'If she's opposed to the idea, she's going to be opposed to it whenever I tell her. So I'd rather get the operation out of the way first, and then tell her.'

I email Dave. I say that I think Casey should tell his mother. Dave's response is this: 'Although he's nearly 24 years old, and not a child, I can understand that it sounds cowardly, and maybe inconsiderate, not to tell her ahead of time. However, I'm the LEADER of this sinister little cult, and I am not telling relatives because they reacted so strongly when I first mentioned it. It's just a nuisance when people start raving and treating you like you've lost your mind. If it would make YOU feel better, I think he would probably agree to telling her. It's only three weeks now until he donates, so it'll have to be pretty soon. I personally would feel better if she DID know, so it won't be so much of a shock when she finds out afterwards, as long as she does not try to make problems with the hospital where the transplant is taking place. See, in our case, she would only need to phone and say he's part of a religious "cult" – the magic C word – and the operation would probably be off.'

A few days later, Casey decides to test the water with a chatty email to his mother. 'It was full of mundane things,' he tells me. 'Small talk. How are her days going? And I just mentioned in the email that I'm thinking of donating a kidney. I haven't heard anything yet.'

'How do you think she'll respond?' I ask.

'She may have the impression that I'm being coerced,' he says.

'Does she feel that way about the Jesus Christians, anyway?' I ask.

'She does feel conflicted by our unity.'

'That you're a live-in group?'

'That we hold ourselves accountable to each other. We make group decisions. It isn't the kind of personal freedom she feels I should have, I guess.'

During the pre-op psychological tests, the doctors soon realized that Robin and Casey's altruism was part of a group scheme. 'Will your Christian friends think less of you if you don't donate?' they asked.

'No,' said Robin.

'What if you have an accident in later life?' asked the doctors. 'Maybe you'll need your spare kidney in the future.'

'The Bible says we must step out in faith,' replied Robin. 'We must do the good we can do today and not wait until tomorrow.'

They were given questionnaires. They had to tick the statements that they felt most applied to them: 'I hear voices most of the time'; 'I feel I have a tight band around my head most of the time'; 'I've always wanted to be a girl'. The doctors told them to answer honestly, because they had ways of telling if they were lying.

'I don't hear voices, but I do get stressed out,' Casey tells me. 'But they don't provide little boxes where you can explain these things.' Casey is feeling stressed out, in part because he feels the process is taking too long. 'I wish it would all go quicker because I'm pretty committed,' he says.

They passed the tests. The hospital warned that 'even a hint of publicity' would result in the operations being abandoned. I send Casey and Robin a video camera, to film the trip to Minneapolis.

That night, I receive an anxious email from Dave in Australia: 'Jon, I am taking a big risk by sharing this with you before we have donated. Even the slightest leak could sabotage the entire project.'

A flurry of emails follows from Dave, more than sixty in all. Sometimes they are chatty. Often they are tense: 'You and I both know that the idea of a "cult" donating kidneys en masse is a "sensational" story. Susan said that you were talking like you still suspect that members are being coerced into donating, that they are getting paid for donations, and that the money is going to me. She said that she thought you were quite nervous about being seen with her placing the business cards in waiting rooms. You've asked us some hard questions, so I think it's time for us to ask you a few. ARE you thinking of writing something nasty about us?'

Sometimes, Dave seems to regret letting me in on the secret and I begin to wonder why he did. Does he have a plan for me that I'm not aware of? Am I a pawn in some grander scheme of his? Yes – I soon discover – I am.

Dave McKay is a fifty-seven-year-old native of Rochester, New York. He was born into a family of Nazarene Christians. He married young, moved to Australia in 1968, and joined the Children of God sect that was famous for 'flirty fishing' (dispatching attractive female members into the secular world to have sex with potential recruits). They preached the virtue and practice of paedophilia, too. Dave was horrified by their sexual teachings, so he split from the Children of God and formed the Jesus Christians in 1982.

Dave has always admired martyrs who behave provocatively – the Buddhists who set themselves on fire to protest the war in Vietnam, and so on. In fact, he once considered setting himself on fire, in India, when a local orphanage was threatened with closure. More recently, when Abu Sayyaf guerrillas took twenty-five people hostage in the Philippines, Dave offered himself in their place, and tried to set up an international hostage-exchange programme, in which philanthropic Christians would swap places with hostages at a moment's notice. 'I think they were just spiritual tests to ascertain whether I'd be willing to take such extreme steps,' he tells me. 'We don't want to sound a trumpet about how great we are, especially when we haven't actually done anything – at least, not yet.'

Like most people, I first heard of the Jesus Christians on 14 July 2000, when they were splashed over the front page of the *Daily Express* – 'Cult Kidnap Boy Aged 16'. Susan and her husband Roland had apparently spirited away a sixteen-year-old boy called Bobby Kelly from Romford High Street, Essex. Bobby had picked up a Jesus Christians cartoon book outside Marks & Spencer. Within hours, he had forsaken his possessions and moved in with the group. The police were called. The airports and docks were put on the highest alert. The Jesus Christians were suddenly – in the eyes of the authorities and media, tabloids, broadsheets and television news alike – a sinister, brainwashing, child-kidnapping religious cult, under the spell of their charismatic leader.

There was an emergency High Court action to 'rescue' the boy, which led to Bobby's photo being circulated. That's when the Jesus Christians panicked and went on the run, with Bobby in tow. They became fugitives for two weeks. (It was a rather provincial run: they went to Hounslow because it has free parking, to Heston service station for nightly showers and to a campsite on the Surrey–Hampshire border.) When the Jesus Christians tried to put their side of the story to Radio 4's *Today*, an injunction was taken out forbidding the BBC from broadcasting the interview.

'Isn't that classic!' wrote Dave at the time on his website. 'Now that our critics have succeeded in slandering our name all over Britain, they want to gag us. And yet some people still tell us that we should have blind faith in the British system of justice! No, something is very wrong here.'

The scandal ended peacefully. Bobby was found safe and well at a campsite, and was made a ward of court. I interviewed him soon after. He spoke highly of the Jesus Christians, and it became clear to me that some of the reporting was biased and verging on the hysterical. This is why Dave decided – a year later – to give me the story on the kidney endeavour.

It is mid-February 2002. Dave tells me that he has invented a woman called Anita Foster and has created an email account for her. The fictitious Anita is writing to influential anti-cult groups in the UK, such as Reachout Trust and Catalyst. She says she's a concerned mother whose son has joined the Jesus Christians, and could they offer advice. Reachout Trust sends Anita their Jesus Christians fact-file. Dave sends it on to me. Under 'Obsession With Death', it quotes passages from Dave's pamphlets: 'Fear of death is what gives the bosses their power! How long do you think you can survive without eating? Maybe a month or two! OK. Would you rather have one month of freedom or a lifetime of slavery? Anything that isn't worth dying for isn't worth living for ... If you'd like to be part of this army of martyrs, then please write to us today.'

The emails between Anita and the anti-cult groups are getting chattier, Dave tells me. She's a likeable concerned mother. He says Anita will soon take on a pivotal role in this story – she will be the one to leak the kidney scandal to the anti-cult groups. This is Dave's plan: the fictitious Anita's fictitious son will donate a fictitious kidney; Anita will inform the anti-cult groups and imply that Dave is coercing his followers to sell their kidneys on the black market, and that the money will go to him. They will tell the tabloids, and the tabloids will go into a week-long frenzy about the self-mutilating kidney cult. Then – and here's my role in the grand scheme – I'll arrive on the scene with the true story of the Jesus Christians' remarkable philanthropy.

It seems a funny scheme, and one that has the capacity to backfire in myriad ways. What if the anti-cult groups don't believe 'Anita'? What if the tabloids decide that mass kidney-donating is a noble and heroic thing? What if I write unkindly about the group? Why does Dave want to make himself seem more sinister than he actually is?

'Your article will be like the resurrection,' says Dave. 'But the crucifixion is the key thing. If we have to get crucified for the message to get out, that's fine. And you'll be the resurrection.'

Dave begins emailing me stern directives: 'You DON'T HAVE TO BE THE DEVIL'S ADVOCATE on this one. We can let the tabloids do that for us. We want them to have egg on their faces.'

I email back. I tell Dave that I don't feel comfortable with his plan. I feel as if I'm being controlled.

Our relationship descends into an irascible silence. I'm sure there's something philanthropic about his intention to donate a kidney. I'm certain that Robin, Casey, Susan and the others have charitable motives. But when Dave emails me the details of his Machiavellian plot for media control – the Anita Foster leak, the ensuing tabloid frenzy and then me cleaning it all up – I realize he's also seeking revenge for his treatment over the Bobby Kelly incident.

And, it occurs to me, Dave has scheduled the leak for mid-March, after Robin and Casey's operations, but before he, Susan and the other Jesus Christians will have time to give their kidneys. Will the tabloid frenzy – if it occurs – scupper these plans?

'What if you become known as such a sinister cult that nobody wants your kidneys any more?' I ask him.

'Yeah, we've considered that,' he replies. 'I think the biggest concern, as Christians, is that we get the message out. Donating kidneys, for us, is really a minor thing. If we can't do it, we can't.'

'It's a big deal for the recipients,' I snap.

There is a short silence.

'Yeah,' says Dave. 'Um. I'm sure we could, uh, still find ways. We could go to another hospital. We could give false names . . .'

At the Internet cafe in Sutton, Susan is checking her emails again. There are a few from C in Scotland, with whom Susan now corresponds on an almost daily basis. C has told Susan that she doesn't need a kidney immediately, and has suggested that if someone comes along with a more urgent need, Susan should give her kidney to them instead.

'I think that's excellent,' says Susan. 'A really good attitude.'

She reads from C's latest: 'Hey, never mind, I'm sure I'll survive, and even if I don't, that's no big deal either. You might think it seems a bit flippant on my part not to value my life, and I'm not getting all morbid on you – smiley face – it's just that I believe if your time is up, it's up, and there's nothing you can do about it. Anyway, I hope you are well and continue to feel the way you do about donation of organs. I find your attitude most interesting and refreshing.'

'That's very touching,' says Susan. '"When your time's up, it's up." She seems to have faced that reality and has a good attitude about it. I really like her.'

The problem is that Susan has also become friends with another potential recipient: Larry, in Aspen, Colorado. 'I would gladly pay for your transportation to the US, all expenses,' he emailed her. 'It is not legal to sell a kidney, but a good-Samaritan donation might be acceptable. Your gift would be a miracle. God bless you.'

Susan says she's over the moon, but how to choose?

'They both seem so nice,' she says.

So she decides to write a list of questions to both C

and Larry – 'How long have you been on dialysis?' 'What does your doctor think about the chances of you surviving a transplant operation?' And other questions, too: 'Do you drink?' 'Do you smoke?' She sends off the questions.

It is, of course, the DoH's ruling about altruistic kidney donations that has forced her into playing the role of the regulatory authority – or playing the role of an even higher authority than that. Susan is likeable, intelligent and well-meaning. Yet I can't help thinking that, whichever way this story unfolds, some people are going to get hurt.

I begin to think of the story that had been handed to me as a poisoned chalice. I am, in part, supportive of the Jesus Christians' scheme. But I feel queasy about the decision Susan has to make, and I feel queasy about Casey. He may be saving a life, but he's only twenty-three, has been a follower for just a year and still hasn't told his mother. I email Dave to suggest Casey should be given a cooling-off period – perhaps two months away from the group before the operation.

I'm surprised to receive a friendly response.

'Thanks for being so frank,' writes Dave. 'How about we give Casey a couple of months away from the group to cool off?'

I email back to ask if he's serious about this. He

responds a few days later. Events have moved on, he says. Casey has now told his mother everything, and she has fully endorsed his decision: 'Now that Casey's mother is in agreement, there really should be no objection from anyone else. Like, he's almost 24, has lived on his own for several years, has covered his body with tattoos and body-piercings without objections from his parents, and now that he has finally got his life together, he wants to do something really good with it by offering a kidney. If his parents are happy with it, then I don't see any reason why we should tell him to run away and think about it.'

At the end of February, the video diary I asked Robin and Casey to film arrives. It is extraordinarily moving and vivid. It begins with them running at a track in Dallas. They run each morning. This is the day before they fly to Minneapolis. The thing that strikes me most are their smiles. Robin, especially, is always smiling.

Now Robin and Casey are having a snowball fight outside the hospital. Now they're in twin beds at a Days Inn next to the hospital. Robin addresses the camera: 'I'm two days away from donating a kidney to someone I've never met before. The reason I'm doing this comes from my personal belief in God. I guess there are a few hard questions – you're probably wondering if I've thought about them. What happens if I donate a kidney to someone and it gets rejected? Obviously, I wouldn't feel very happy about that. However, part of the idea of being an altruistic donor is that it's a pure act of love. It's like a donation to the human race. And that's all I have to say about that for the moment.'

The camera clicks off.

It clicks back on again. Robin is still smiling. 'Most kidney donations come from cadavers,' he says. 'The recipient has to race in as quickly as possible. They all wear beepers. As soon as they're beeped, they race to the hospital. The working life expectancy of a kidney harvested from a dead person is ten years, whereas a kidney from a live donor lasts at least twenty years. Twenty years is a long time. That's a lease of life.'

Now they are at the hospital, having last-minute electrocardiograms and chest X-rays. Casey strips to his waist. 'What's this 777 mean?' asks the nurse, pointing to one of Casey's many tattoos.

'It's supposed to be the Lord's number,' says Casey. 'The opposite of 666.' He laughs. 'I was too young to think about what I was doing.'

The nurse says, 'You're a brave man, Casey.'

Now, suddenly, it is the night before the operation. Robin and Casey are back at the hotel, preparing their super-laxative. 'So when the surgeons get in there and move our guts around, there won't be any accidents', Robin explains. The super-laxative is called Go Lightly.

They need to drink half a gallon, one glass every ten minutes, 'Until our watery stool is clear and free of solid matter,' says Robin. It's pineapple-flavoured. They say 'Cheers!' and start drinking.

Casey screws up his face. 'It's really bad,' he says.

'We'll get there, buddy,' says Robin. He pats Casey lightly on the knee.

Casey takes another sip. 'I feel like I'm defiling myself,' he says.

Now it's 5.20 a.m. on 21 February 2002. 'We should be leaving,' says Robin. 'Sounds like Casey's still in the shower. I'm feeling a bit dehydrated from the diarrhoea. I guess they could put me on an IV or something. I got a call last night from the doctor. He said I have an unusual structure. He said there's a chance they'll have to go in through the back, which means it's a longer and more difficult recovery. They may have to remove one of the ribs for access.'

'How do you feel about that?' asks Christine, Robin's wife, from behind the camera. Christine is also a Jesus Christian.

'OK, I guess,' replies Robin.

Casey pops his head around the bathroom door and grins. Now they head off, in the snow and the dawn, towards their operations. Now they are in the pre-op room.

'I'm debating whether to keep my eyes open when they put the knockout drug into me,' says Casey.

He's sitting on a chair, his body covered in a tight stocking, like a leotard. 'I keep trying to focus on the spiritual side of this,' says Casey. His voice is small. 'The motivation behind the donation. The benefits of it. Yeah. I'm trying to stay in touch with the One who's making it all possible.'

'Do you have any doubts?' asks Christine.

'I'm just, uh, trying to stay open to what God wants,' says Casey.

Now, from his bed in the pre-op room, Casey tries to phone his mother to tell her that he's about to go into theatre. But she's not there. The phone just rings out. Casey hangs up.

Now the hospital porters arrive. There are hugs from Christine. Robin and Casey are wheeled away towards the operating theatre. The camera clicks off. When it comes back on again, Casey and Robin are just beginning to stir from the anaesthetic. Casey is mumbling incoherently. Christine is stroking his arm. There are drips, and bandages cover their stomachs. The camera clicks off.

'I'm feeling very dizzy and nauseous,' says Casey – his voice is hazy, as if he's still in a dream. It is the next morning. 'I just vomited up some gastric juice or something. You wanna come and have a look at my wound?

The pain medication is making it really itchy. I keep scratching. You want to see me press my morphine button? Ah!'

'That's my buddy,' says Robin. The camera clicks off.

The days progress. Casey tries walking, but he has to sit down again. His colon is twisted from the operation. For a while he lies under the duvet cover. He says that he doesn't want to talk to anyone, and he wants Christine to stop filming him. He says he wishes he hadn't done it.

'I keep asking myself, why did I donate?' he says. 'I was trying to do something good and this pain is what I get for it. Maybe God is having me go through this trial to make me feel more sensitive to other people who are uncomfortable and in pain. I have to be careful not to become hateful or bitter. That's what I'm working on now.'

The next day, Casey and Robin are wheeled out into the sunshine. 'We heard a little bit about the recipients today,' says Robin. 'My kidney went to a fifty-nine-year-old man who's been a diabetic all his life. So the fact that he's fifty-nine and he hasn't needed a transplant until now is an indication that he's been looking after himself. Apparently, it's going really well for him. The kidney began producing urine straight away. Tell them about your recipient, Casey.'

There is a short silence. Casey seems happier today.

'My recipient was a fifty-three-year-old woman who had been on dialysis for five years,' he says. 'Her time was nearly up. Hopefully, she doesn't have to worry about that any more.' Then he adds, 'A lot of people pray to God for a miracle, specifically relating to kidney failure, and all it takes is someone to step forward and say, "I'll do it." That's the miracle. That willingness to step forward. That's God's miracle. We don't have to sit around waiting for God to do all the work. He's waiting for us to do something.'

'We can make a miracle happen,' says Robin.

On 15 March, I receive an email from Dave McKay. He's decided to kill off Anita. He realized that attempting to control the tabloids and the anti-cult groups was bound to backfire.

'I know we're going to cop it sometime. We just wanted to have control over when we cop it. I just wanted to show how adept the media is at turning something good into something evil.'

Dave says that Casey and Robin are recovering well. Casey's had regrets, but now he's pulling out of it and is glad of his decision again. Susan's relationships with C in Scotland and Larry in Colorado continue to flourish. She hopes to donate to one or other of them as soon as she can. Dave hopes to donate within a few weeks, at a hospital in Australia.

He says the hospital in Minneapolis has given Robin and Casey's address to their two recipients, but neither has written to thank them.

Postscript

Dave McKay hated the story. He *hated* it. I'd been filming the group for a Channel 4 documentary and the moment Dave read the article he pulled the plug on the filming.

He said he wanted me to think about what I had done.

I didn't know what he meant. I thought the story was fine. I'd spent about £40,000 of Channel 4's money, and now Dave had pulled the plug on the filming.

For the next three months or so, Dave consumed my life. He kept saying I had to think about what I'd done.

I needed to find a way to continue filming, so I began to suggest things I had possibly done wrong.

'Mentioning the whole Anita Foster thing?' I emailed to ask.

Dave's mysterious, cold antipathy turned into rage. He began emailing long, furious explanations of what I had done wrong. Scores of emails arrived, containing line-by-line analyses of all that was bad about my story.

How I was always looking for cheap laughs or scandal. How I was more insidious than a tabloid cult-buster. At least you knew where you stood with the tabloids. I buried my attacks in clever, sneaky little phrases like, 'There is a silence.'

The Jesus Christians were saving lives. I was attacking them with nasty sarcasm and underhand belittling tactics.

Why – Dave asked – did I go on about Casey's brief regrets when he was recovering from the operation?

'A woman in labour probably regrets ever getting pregnant,' he emailed.

These emails from Dave arrived almost every day for months. I began to wish he would donate both his kidneys. I'd open my inbox each morning with a knot in my stomach. The emails read like admonishments from a teacher, like I should feel grateful that even though Dave was at the end of his tether he was still taking the time and trouble to point out my faults to me.

He hated the line about the poisoned chalice, and read it out sarcastically in a video message he sent me: ' "*I begin to think of the story that has been handed to me as a poisoned chalice. I feel queasy about the decision Susan has to make and I feel queasy about Casey.*" So why did you write the story, Jon? It was your poisoned chalice and you drank from it with GUSTO.'

No tabloid frenzy ensued as a result of my story appearing, only an article in a local paper called the *Catford News Shopper*.

'You are only reaping what you have sown,' Dave emailed, referring to the trouble I was in now he'd cancelled the filming. 'Welcome to the real world. Love, Dave.'

After a few months of this I began to agree with Dave's criticisms of me.

I agreed especially with his criticism that the line ' "It's a big deal for the recipients," I snap' was intensely annoying, as it was erroneously presenting me as some kind of journalistic knight in shining armour. Eventually Dave and I agreed that if I pledged to publicly apologize in the documentary for what I had written in the *Guardian* I would be allowed to continue filming.

'An apology is a GREAT idea!' Dave emailed to say.

I met up with Roland, one of the London-based leaders of the Jesus Christians. He drafted an impromptu apology for me to read out in the documentary.

'It would be great,' Roland said, 'if you could say something like, "Hello, I'm Jon Ronson. I really must apologize for my article. I said this . . . Blah blah blah . . . It was wrong. And I guess I've been doing it for many years – reading into things or trying to make them more exciting – and in my zeal I misrepresented a few things. And I apologize." '

Many years? I thought.

I didn't say anything. I had been rather admonished into submission by then.

Roland said he thought Dave was 'extremely patient' with me when it came to pointing out my faults.

'I was marvelling at the amount of time he took over it,' he said.

'It certainly took many emails from Dave for me to see the error of my ways,' I said.

'It was worth it,' Roland said.

A month or so earlier, Roland's wife Susan had gone to visit C in Scotland, and I went with her. This was the woman with kidney failure Susan had been corresponding with by email, along with Larry in Aspen.

C turned out to be a young woman called Christine.

'When I first read the email,' Christine told me when Susan was out of earshot, 'I thought, "nutter". A part of me still thinks there has to be some catch. But as yet I've not sussed it out. And maybe there isn't one. Maybe it's just my untrusting nature. She doesn't seem like a crazy, off-her-head person. She seems like a normal sane person. So she obviously knows what she's doing. She hasn't been brainwashed, as far as you can make out. It's what she believes. And everyone's entitled to their own beliefs, right? What's the group called?'

'The Jesus Christians,' I said.

'I've not heard of them,' she said.

'They've never been that successful,' I said, 'because they aren't the most fun religious cult to be in.'

'It doesn't sound like it if you have to give a bit of your body away to join,' Christine shrugged. We laughed.

Now, Roland told me, Susan had decided not to donate her kidney to Christine, but to Larry in Aspen. The decision came to her in a dream, which she took to be a message from God. In the dream, she met a sixty-year-old man with grey hair, a little overweight, and he was happy to see her because she was about to give him her kidney. That's exactly what Larry looked like, which is why she took this dream to be a message from God.

A few weeks passed. Then I received an email from Dave in Australia. He wrote that Christine from Scotland was dying. He said he *could* instruct one of his members to give her a kidney, but if he did I would only accuse him of manipulation. So instead, he wrote, he had decided to let Christine die and let her death be on my conscience.

He posted me a video message. It was him, sitting on a sofa, speaking directly into the camera.

'It's one thirty in the morning here in Australia,' he said, 'and I've just received an urgent telephone call from the UK. It seems that Christine in Scotland has had a turn for the worse and I have to make a decision immediately if we're going to help her at all. At the moment the only person in the community available to help Christine is Reinhart, and he's booked to fly to India tomorrow morning. The problem with Reinhart is that although he's willing to donate, he's not very keen. I could push him into it. I have to make a decision, and there's a life dependent on it.'

Dave paused. The bags under his eyes practically reached down to the end of his nose. His beard looked stragglier than ever.

'The decision I make,' he said, 'is going to have to take into consideration repercussions from the media – people like yourself. As you know we stopped the filming after your article appeared in the *Guardian*. Amongst other things I was upset about the fact that you portrayed me as a manipulator, forcing or coercing Casey into doing something he might later regret. I think that was terribly unfair both to Casey and myself. No way did I push him into doing it. I didn't even approach him. It was his idea and he ran with it. And that's why we decided not to cooperate with you. But after this phone call tonight I've had a rethink. I'm prepared to go ahead with the documentary, but on one condition: you use this video. You see, I'm not going to say anything to Reinhart. I'll let him fly out tomorrow. And I'll let Christine's blood be on your head, and on the heads of the authorities there in England, those people who felt that because a group of Christians wanted to donate their kidneys to strangers, there was something wrong with us. So go ahead. Make your documentary. But don't forget to tell them about the recipients. That's the big picture, Jon, and that's been overlooked. These recipients are real people. People like Christine.'

Dave bowed his head and said: 'Thank you.'

You stupid fucking idiot, I thought.

I'd entered Dave's world convinced that the cult-busters were the crazy ones, comparing Dave to *Invasion of the Body Snatchers*, etc. But now I thought of him that way. Why? Because I really didn't like him. I began to dislike Dave enormously, irrationally, in the way that former members of sects hate their former leaders after they rejoin the real world.

Dave had especially hated the implication in my article that he was personally hoping to get out of donating a kidney. And, as it transpired, Dave did indeed donate one, in January 2003, to a man from California.

Susan donated a kidney to Larry from Aspen. I don't know what happened to Christine from Scotland. Three years later, on 26 April 2006, the Department of Health announced plans to legalize altruistic kidney donations – donations from a stranger to a stranger – as long as they were assured no money was changing hands, and no coercion was taking place.

In the winter of 2005 I was walking through Dalston, East London, when I bumped into Roland, Susan's husband. Roland was always my favourite Jesus Christian. I liked him even when he was drafting that apology for me to read out in my documentary. So it was nice to see him. We shook hands.

'How are you?' I asked.

'I've been . . . mmm . . . Kenyan prison . . . mmm . . . tepee . . .' whispered Roland.

I remembered what an unusually quiet talker Roland was.

'Sorry?' I said.

I leaned in and put my ear right next to his mouth.

'I've just been released from a Kenyan prison,' Roland repeated. 'They falsely accused me of kidnapping someone and now I've got TB.'

OK, I thought. What do I know about TB?

I reached around in my memory and found a photograph of World War One soldiers all dying of it in a quarantined hospital.

Right, I thought. That means TB *is* contagious.

'I'm suing the Kenyan government,' Roland said, 'for false imprisonment.'

OK, I thought. How far is my ear from his mouth? About an inch. Should I assume that TB is an airborne virus? Yes, it is prudent to presume that. Can it therefore be caught via the ear? Yes.

'My TB is contained now but I was coughing up blood and mucus,' Roland said.

Now, I thought, what is the etiquette regarding jumping terrified away from someone with TB? Is it offensive to do so?

I gracefully edged my ear away from his mouth.

The thing is, I thought, the Jesus Christians hate me. They once called me a Christ-hating Jew. Might Roland be exacting revenge on behalf of the sect by deliberately breathing TB into my ear?

I spotted a Boots across the road.

OK, I thought. I'm going to say goodbye, walk causally up the street and then, when I'm sure Roland's not looking, I'll double back, rush into Boots and tell the pharmacist what just happened.

So I did.

'I've just shaken hands with someone with TB,' I practically shouted.

The pharmacist – inappropriately, I thought – burst

out laughing. Maybe she didn't realize how close the contact was.

'He didn't cough on me but he breathed in my ear,' I explained.

She laughed even harder.

'He's a member of a religious sect,' I explained, 'who forsake all possessions, which might mean he isn't as clean as he ought to be.'

She was screaming with laughter now.

'Do you think I should get some antiseptic wipes?' I asked.

'If you think it'll bring you peace of mind,' she replied.

There was a silence.

'Can one use antiseptic wipes on the ear?' I asked.

There really was a time – in the months after my article appeared – when I began to agree with Dave's criticisms of me. When I suggested apologizing in the film for all I had done wrong in the article, it wasn't just to get Dave off my back. It wasn't just to make the emails stop and the filming resume. It was also because somehow, by attrition, or by technique, Dave had managed to make something click in my brain. It only really clicked back again when he sent me that absurd, nasty message about letting Christine die and letting her death be on my conscience. That was Dave over-egging the pudding wildly, and it brought me back to my senses. But for a while back then I can honestly say I had fallen victim to a kind of mean-spirited, cack-handed mind control.

I told Elaine at the time. I said, 'I'm honestly thinking of apologizing in the film, because I can no longer tell if I'm right or wrong. I think Dave's right. But I don't know. Maybe he is right. Or maybe he's manipulating my thoughts.'

'So,' Elaine replied, 'you're saying you might have fallen victim to a cult leader's mind-control spell?'

'Yes!' I said.

Elaine mumbled something about me being prone to over-dramatic theatrics. I mumbled something about her proclivity to judge people when she isn't in full possession of the facts. And really she should try and step into my shoes and see what it feels like. Elaine said it is ridiculous to think someone can mind-control someone. I said I used to believe that too.

Luckily, I had a handy way of finding out if I was indeed being mind-controlled. I went to my bookcase and rifled around for the pamphlet *Cults: A Practical Guide* by Ian Haworth. He was in a cult once. His cult believed they could breathe underwater and were immortal. Ian didn't last long because he nearly killed himself underwater. Now he's one of Britain's leading anti-cult activists.

I leafed through the pamphlet until I reached the chapter 'What is Mind Control?'. It includes a checklist of twenty-six mind-control techniques (Hypnosis, Peer Group Pressure, Love Bombing, etc). Of the twenty-six, I had, I worked out, fallen victim to about twelve. Well, some were definites like 'Verbal Abuse: Desensitizing through bombardment with foul and abusive language'. Others I wasn't entirely certain about, like 'Metacommunication: Implanting subliminal messages by stressing certain key words or phrases in long, confusing lectures'. Dave might not have been doing that. But I stuck it in my list anyway, to bolster numbers. Elaine continued to think I was being over-dramatic about Dave and his mind-control techniques.

A few months passed. Then, one day, we were expelled from the small private primary school we had sent our then five-year-old son Joel to.

He had been in the school for two terms. It had seemed lovely at first.

The teachers had photographs of themselves as children tacked up on their brightly coloured classroom doors.

That's so nice! I thought.

The headmistress (I'll call her Jenny) said, 'Call me Jenny! I insist the children call me Jenny!'

So we sent off our cheque and a few weeks later we received our acceptance letter: 'We look forward very much to the pleasure of teaching Gerald,' the letter began.

Gerald? I thought. Joel is four and not a billionaire property magnate.

'Rest assured that we will always have the children's best interests at heart,' the letter continued. 'Please never hesitate to contact us if you have any queries at any time. Communication is a keyword in our relationship. Don't be afraid to ask.'

Things were fine for the first term. Joel became a freakishly good reader and writer. Hours on end were spent tracing letters and numbers. He had the writing skills of a six-year-old. But all that tracing meant the children weren't getting to play with each other enough. I mentioned this to some of the other parents and they said, 'Yes, yes, but the children will fly through their entrance exams for the City of London or St Paul's. Isn't that what matters?'

One of the school's great selling points was its proximity to some beautiful old private gardens. The prospectus promised that the children would play in them three times a week. After the Christmas holidays, the children abruptly stopped playing in the gardens.

'Why aren't they letting you out to play?' I asked Joel, when he happened to mention it to us.

'Jenny doesn't want her new carpet to get muddy,' he replied, solemnly.

Instead, the fifty or so younger children spent their lunchtimes down in the basement where, Joel said, 'We're not allowed to run, but they do let me hop a bit.'

We stared, startled, at Joel.

'It is fun when they let us play with the blocks,' he said, conciliatorily.

(Actually, Joel later told us, the hopping was wishful thinking on his part, and that hopping was in fact outlawed in the basement.)

We weren't afraid to ask.

'Did you see how muddy the carpet got last term?' asked Jenny.

She explained this was a temporary measure, and the children would be out playing again after the half term.

It didn't happen. The mid-February weather was unusually beautiful. There was no mud. The children were going to school in T-shirts, but still spending their lunchtimes in the basement.

On the second morning of the heat wave, Elaine asked Jenny, sharply, when the children might get out to play, and Jenny reiterated her muddy-carpet fears.

On the third day Elaine picked Joel up from school at lunchtime and took him out to the gardens for a play, which did not go down well with the school.

On the fourth morning, Jenny was waiting at the door.

'It's a beautiful day,' said Elaine.

'Yes it is,' said Jenny.

'Will the children be out in the gardens today?' asked Elaine.

'Don't you dare tell me how to run my school,' said Jenny.

Inside the classroom another mother asked Jenny about the garden.

'If you don't like the way I run my school,' replied Jenny, in front of the class, 'then you can take your child out.'

The next morning, we – and the other mother – received identical letters from Jenny. They read, 'Further to our discussion this morning it is quite clear that you do not recognize and appreciate the values we hold at this school. Please accept this letter as one term's notice that we will expect your child to leave the school at the end of the current school year. Please note that if you leave before the end of the summer term you will forfeit your deposit.'

We had been expelled.

The other mother went to see a solicitor, who said he heard stories like this all the time. There's very little you can do to protect yourself against a private school with no board of governors and no trustees, he said.

We decided to apologize to Jenny for disrespecting the values she holds dear, in the hope that she might de-expel Joel, which would give us enough time to find him another school.

At the meeting between Jenny and Elaine the next afternoon Jenny said, 'I've got a list of clients as long as my arm dying to send their children here.'

Elaine started to cry.

'I watch you from the window,' said Jenny. 'I see you talking to the other parents, and it worries me.'

'I'm just an over-anxious parent,' said Elaine.

'If you have problems,' said Jenny, in a sweet voice, 'come and see me and we can sit on the sofa and have a little therapy session. You know, there was one father who needed a little therapy session nearly every day for a long time! But he finally came to accept that the decisions I make are in the best interests of the school as a whole! And his children are still here!'

Elaine began to realize that the letters of expulsion were just a warning shot, and one designed to be heard by all the parents.

'When you drop your child off at the door he becomes our responsibility,' said Jenny, 'and you have to accept that. Do you think you can accept that?'

Elaine sniffled and nodded. Jenny passed her a Kleenex.

'Well, let's see you come in tomorrow morning with a happy smile on your face!' said Jenny. 'Show the other mothers that whatever problems there have been are sorted out. Can you do that?'

Elaine nodded.

Later that week, Elaine was walking down the street when a woman in a Mercedes pulled over. She rolled down her window.

'I'm really sorry,' she said. 'I heard what happened and I really wanted to support you. But when I told my husband, he said, "For God's sake don't you say anything or we'll get a letter like that."'

Elaine later said to me that her submissive behaviour inside Jenny's office was just a show, so Jenny would de-expel Joel, which would give us enough time to find a new school for him. But later still she said that something had clicked in her brain when she was in the office that day, just like something had clicked in my brain during the months I was receiving the torrent of emails from Dave McKay.

Joel now goes to a state primary school a few streets away from us. A little while after we moved him, I bumped into a father from the old school. He said the good news was that the children are getting out to play in the square every day, 'until Jenny gets back from her round-the-world trip'.

'Every day?' I said. 'Won't Jenny be furious when she finds out?'

'What school is Joel in now?' he asked.

I told him.

'How much is it costing?'

'Nothing,' I said.

He looked shocked.

'Isn't it full of . . .?' He trailed off. Then he put his thumbs in his jacket in an imitation of someone doing the Lambeth Walk.

I tried to explain, but he didn't really want to know.

In *Cults: A Practical Guide*, Ian Haworth writes that mind-control techniques include:

- Finger Pointing: Creating a false sense of righteousness by pointing to the shortcomings of the outside world.

'What school is Joel in now?' the father from the old school asked me.

I told him.

'How much is it costing?' he asked.

'Nothing,' I said.

He looked shocked.

'Isn't it full of . . .?' He trailed off. Then he put his thumbs in his jacket in an imitation of someone doing the Lambeth Walk.

- Flaunting Hierarch: Promoting acceptance of cult authority by promising advancement, power and salvation.

'The children will fly through their entrance exams for the City of London or St Paul's.'

- No Questions: Accomplishing automatic acceptance of beliefs by discouraging questions.

'When you drop your child off at the door he becomes our responsibility, and you have to accept that. Do you think you can accept that?'

- Love Bombing: Creating a sense of family and belonging through hugging, kissing, touching and flattery.

'If you have problems, come and see me and we can sit on the sofa and have a little therapy session. You know, there was one father who needed a little therapy session nearly every day for a long time! But he finally came to accept that the decisions I make are in the best interests of the school as a whole! And his children are still here!'

- Disinhibition: Encouraging child-like obedience by orchestrating child-like behaviour.

'Well, let's see you come in tomorrow morning with a happy smile on your face! Show the other mothers that

whatever problems there have been are sorted out. Can you do that?'

I don't mean to suggest that the private primary school was a cult. In fact I think our experience with the school should be seen as a defence of Dave McKay and the Jesus Christians, and the other religious sects often dismissed as bizarre, dangerous cults by the media. We imagine this sort of manipulative, zealous behaviour taking place only on the fringes of our society, when in fact I suspect it routinely occurs to everyone all the time: inside offices, schools and families.

9. CITIZEN KUBRICK

In 1996 I received what was and probably remains the most exciting telephone call I've ever had. It was from a man calling himself Tony.

'I'm phoning on behalf of Stanley Kubrick,' he said.

'I'm sorry?' I said.

'Stanley would like you to send him a radio documentary you made called *Hotel Auschwitz*,' said this man. This was a programme I had made for BBC Radio 4 about the marketing of the concentration camp.

'Stanley Kubrick?' I said.

'Let me give you the address,' said the man. He sounded posh. It seemed that he didn't want to say any more about this than he had to. I sent the tape to a PO box in St Albans and I waited. What might happen next? Whatever it was, it was going to be amazing. My mind started going crazy. Perhaps Kubrick would ask me to collaborate on something. (Oddly, in this daydream, I reluctantly turned him down because I didn't think I'd make a good screenwriter.)

By the time I received that telephone call, nine years had passed since Kubrick's last film – *Full Metal Jacket*. All anyone outside his circle knew about him was that he was living in a vast country house somewhere near St Albans – or a 'secret lair' according to a *Sunday Times* article of that year – behaving presumably like some kind of mad hermit genius. Nobody even knew what he looked like. It had been sixteen years since a photograph of him had been published.

He'd gone from making a film a year in the 1950s (including the brilliant, horrific *Paths of Glory*), to a film every couple of years in the sixties (*Lolita*, *Dr Strangelove* and *2001* all came out within a six-year period), to two films per decade in the seventies and eighties (there had been a seven-year gap between *The Shining* and *Full Metal Jacket*) and now, in the 1990s, absolutely nothing at all. What the hell was he doing in there? According to rumours, he was passing his time being terrified of germs and refusing to let his chauffeur drive over 30 mph. But now I knew what he was doing. He was listening to my BBC Radio 4 documentary, *Hotel Auschwitz*.

'The good news,' wrote *The Times* that year, bemoaning the ever-lengthening gaps between his films, 'is that Kubrick is reportedly a hoarder. There is apparently an extensive archive of material at his home in Childwick-bury Manor. When that is eventually opened we may get close to understanding the tangled brain which brought to life HAL, the *Clockwork Orange* Droogs and Jack Torrance.'

The thing is, once I sent the tape to the PO box, nothing happened next. I never heard anything again. Not a word. My cassette disappeared into the mysterious world of Stanley Kubrick. And then, three years later, Kubrick was dead.

Two years after that – in 2001 – I got another phone call out of the blue from the man called Tony.

'Do you want to get some lunch?' he asked. 'Why don't you come up to Childwick?'

The journey to the Kubrick house starts normally. You drive through the St Albans suburbs, passing ordi-nary-sized post-war houses and opticians and vets. Then you turn right, past the Private Road sign, into an almost absurdly perfect picturesque model village. Even the name, Childwick Green, sounds like A. A. Milne wrote it. There's an electric gate at the end, with a Do Not Trespass sign. Drive through that, and through some woods, and past a long white fence with the paint peeling off, and then another electric gate, and then another electric gate, and then another electric gate and you're in the middle of an estate full of boxes.

There are boxes everywhere – shelves of boxes in the stable block, rooms full of boxes in the main house. In the fields, where racehorses once stood and grazed, are half a dozen Portakabins, each packed with boxes. These are the boxes that contain the legendary Kubrick archive. Was *The Times* right? Would the stuff inside the boxes offer an understanding of his 'tangled brain'? I notice that many of the boxes are sealed. Some have, in fact, remained unopened for decades.

Tony turns out to be Tony Frewin. He started working as an office boy for Kubrick in 1965, when he was seventeen. One day, apropos of nothing, Kubrick said to him, 'You have that office outside my office if I need you.'

That was thirty-six years ago and Tony is still here, two years after Kubrick died and was buried in the grounds behind the house. There may be no more Kubrick movies to make, but there are DVDs to re-master and reissue in special editions. There are box sets and retrospective books to oversee. There is paperwork.

Tony gives me a guided tour through the house. We walk past boxes and more boxes and filing cabinets and past a grand staircase. Childwick was once home to a family of horse-trainers called the Joels. Back then there was, presumably, busts or floral displays on either side at the bottom of this staircase. Here, instead, is a photocopier on one side and a fax machine on the other.

'This is how Stanley left it,' says Tony.

Stanley Kubrick's house looks like the Inland Revenue took it over long ago.

Tony takes me into a large room painted blue and filled with books.

'This used to be the cinema,' he tells me.

'Is it the library now?' I ask.

'Look closer at the books,' says Tony.

I do.

'Bloody hell,' I say. 'Every book in this room is about *Napoleon*!'

'Look in the drawers,' says Tony.

I do.

'It's all about Napoleon too!' I say. 'Everything in here is about *Napoleon*!'

I must say I feel a little like Shelley Duvall in *The Shining*, chancing upon her husband's novel and finding it is comprised entirely of the line 'All Work And No Play Makes Jack A Dull Boy' typed over and over again. John Baxter wrote, in his unauthorized biography of Kubrick, 'Most people attributed the purchase of Childwick to Kubrick's passion for privacy, and drew parallels with Jack Torrance in *The Shining*.' This room full of Napoleon stuff seems to bear that comparison out.

'Somewhere else in this house,' Tony says, 'is a cabinet full of twenty-five thousand library cards, three inches by five inches. If you want to know what Napoleon, or Josephine, or anyone within Napoleon's inner circle was doing on the afternoon of July 23rd, 17-whatever, you go to that card and it'll tell you.'

'Who made up the cards?' I ask.

'Stanley,' says Tony. 'With some assistants.'

'How long did it take?' I ask.

'Years,' says Tony. 'The late sixties.'

Kubrick never made his film about Napoleon. During the years it took him to compile this research, a Rod Steiger movie called *Waterloo* was written, produced and released. It was a box-office failure, so MGM abandoned *Napoleon* and Kubrick made *A Clockwork Orange* instead.

'Did you do this kind of massive research for all the movies?' I ask Tony.

'More or less,' he says.

'OK,' I say. 'I understand how you might do this for *Napoleon*, but what about, say, *The Shining*?'

'Somewhere here,' says Tony, 'is just about every ghost book ever written, and there'll be a box containing photographs of the exteriors of maybe every mountain hotel in the world.'

There is a silence.

'Tony,' I say. 'Can I look through the boxes?'

I've been coming to the Kubrick house a couple of times a month ever since.

I start, chronologically, in a Portakabin behind the stable block, with a box marked *Lolita*. I open it, noting the ease with which the lid comes off.

These are excellent, well-designed boxes, I think to myself.

I flick through the paperwork inside, pausing randomly at a letter that reads as if it has come straight from a Jane Austen novel:

> *Dear Mr Kubrick,*
> *Just a line to express to you and to Mrs Kubrick*
> *my husband's and my own deep appreciation of*
> *your kindness in arranging for Dimitri's*
> *introduction to your uncle, Mr Guenther Rennert.*
> *Sincerely,*
> *Mrs Vladimir Nabokov*

I later learn that Dimitri was a budding opera singer and Rennert was a famous opera director, in charge of the Munich Opera House and Glyndebourne. This letter was written in 1962, back in the days when Kubrick was still producing a film every year or so. This box is full of fascinating correspondence between Kubrick and the

Nabokovs but – unlike the fabulously otherworldly Napoleon room, which was accrued six years later – it is the kind of stuff you would probably find in any director's archive.

The unusual stuff – the stuff that elucidates the ever-lengthening gaps between productions – can be found in the boxes that were compiled from 1968 onwards. In a box next to the *Lolita* box in the Portakabin I find an unusually terse letter, written by Kubrick to someone called Pat, on 10 January 1968:

> *Dear Pat,*
> *Although you are apparently too busy to*
> *personally return my phone calls, perhaps you will*
> *find time in the near future to reply to this letter?*

(Later, when I show Tony Frewin this letter, he says he's surprised by the brusqueness. Kubrick must have been at the end of his tether, he says, because on a number of occasions he said to Tony, 'Before you send an angry letter, imagine how it would look if it got into the hands of *Time Out*.') The reason for Kubrick's annoyance in this particular letter was because he'd heard that the Beatles were going to use a landscape shot from *Dr Strangelove* in one of their movies.

'The Beatle film will be very widely seen,' Kubrick

writes, 'and it will make it appear that that the material in *Dr Strangelove* is stock footage. I feel this harms the film.'

There are a similar batch of telexes from 1975: 'It would appear', Kubrick writes in one, 'that *Space 1999* may very well become a long-running and important television series. There seems nothing left now but to seek the highest possible damages ... The deliberate choice of a date only two years away from *2001* is not accidental and harms us.'

This telex was written seven years after the release of *2001*.

But you can see why Kubrick sometimes felt compelled to wage war to protect the honour of his work. A 1975 telex, from a picture publicity man at Warner Bros called Mark Kauffman, regards publicity stills for Kubrick's sombre reworking of Thackeray's *Barry Lyndon*. It reads: 'Received additional material. Is there any material with humour or zaniness that you could send?'

Kubrick replies, clearly through gritted teeth: 'The style of the picture is reflected by the stills you have already received. The film is based on William Make-peace Thackeray's novel which, though it has irony and wit, could not be well described as zany.'

I take a break from the boxes to wander over to

Tony's office. As I walk in I notice something pinned onto his letterbox.

'POSTMAN', it reads. 'Please put all mail in the white box under the colonnade across the courtyard to your right.'

It is not a remarkable note except for one thing. The typeface Tony used to print it is exactly the same typeface Kubrick used for the posters and title sequences of *Eyes Wide Shut* and *2001*.

'It's Futura Extra Bold,' explains Tony. 'It was Stanley's favourite typeface. It's sans serif. He liked Helvetica and Univers too. Clean and elegant.'

'Is this the kind of thing you and Kubrick used to discuss?' I ask.

'God, yes,' says Tony. 'Sometimes late into the night. I was always trying to persuade him to turn away from them. But he was wedded to his sans serifs.'

Tony goes to his bookshelf and brings down a number of volumes full of examples of typefaces, the kind of volumes he and Kubrick used to study, and he shows them to me.

'I did once get him to admit the beauty of Bembo,' he adds, 'a serif.'

'So is that note to the postman a sort of private tribute from you to Kubrick?' I ask.

'Yeah,' says Tony. He smiles to himself. 'Yeah, yeah.'

For a moment I also smile at the unlikely image of the two men discussing the relative merits of typefaces late into the night, but then I remember the first time I saw the trailer for *Eyes Wide Shut*, the way the words CRUISE, KIDMAN, KUBRICK flashed dramatically onto the screen in large red, yellow and white colours, to the song 'They Did A Bad, Bad Thing'. Had the words not been in Futura Extra Bold, I realize now, they wouldn't have sent such a chill up the spine. Kubrick and Tony obviously became, at some point during their relationship, tireless amateur sleuths, wanting to amass and consume and understand all information.

But this attention to detail becomes so amazingly evident and seemingly all-consuming in the later boxes, I begin to wonder whether it was worth it. In one Portakabin, for example, there are hundreds and hundreds of boxes marked EWS – Portman Square, EWS – Kensington and Chelsea, etc, etc. I choose the one marked EWS – Islington because that's where I live. Inside are hundreds of photographs of doorways. The doorway of my local video shop, Century Video, is here, as is the doorway of my dry cleaners, Spots Suede Services on Upper Street. Then, as I continue to flick through the photographs, I find to my astonishment pictures of the doorways of the houses in my own street.

Hand-written at the top of these photographs are the words, 'Hooker doorway?'

Huh, I think.

So somebody within the Kubrick organization (it was, in fact, his nephew) once walked up my street, on Kubrick's orders, hoping to find a suitable doorway for a hooker in *Eyes Wide Shut*. It is both an extremely interesting find and a bit of a kick in the teeth.

It is not, though, as incredible a coincidence as it may first seem. Judging by the writing on the boxes, probably just about every doorway in London has been captured and placed inside this Portakabin. This solves one mystery for me – the one about why Kubrick, a native of the Bronx, chose the St Albans countryside, of all places, for his home. I realize now that it didn't matter. It could have been anywhere. It is as if the whole world is to be found somewhere within this estate.

But was it worth it? Was the hooker doorway eventually picked for *Eyes Wide Shut* the quintessential hooker doorway? Back at home I watch *Eyes Wide Shut* again on DVD. The hooker doorway looks exactly like any doorway you would find in Lower Manhattan – maybe on Canal Street or in the East Village. It is a red door, up some brownstone steps, with the number 265 painted on the glass at the top. Tom Cruise is pulled through the door by the hooker. The scene is over in a few seconds.

(It was eventually shot on a set at Pinewood.) I remember the Napoleon archive, the years it took Kubrick and some assistants to compile it, and I suggest to Jan Harlan, Kubrick's executive producer and brother-in-law, that had there not been all those years of attention to detail during the early planning of the movie, perhaps *Napoleon* would have actually been made.

'That's a completely theoretical and obsolete observation!' replies Jan, in a jolly manner. 'That's like saying if Vermeer had painted in a different style he'd have done a hundred more paintings.'

'OK,' I say.

Jan is right, of course. So why am I so keen to discover in the boxes some secret personality flaw to Kubrick, whose films I love so much? He was the greatest director of his generation. Jack Nicholson's 'Here's Johnny!' Lolita's heart-shaped sunglasses. The *Dr Strangelove* cowboy riding the nuclear bomb like it's a bucking bronco. And on and on. So many images have implanted themselves into the public consciousness, surely because of the director's ever-burgeoning attention to detail.

'Why don't you just accept,' says Jan, 'that this was how he worked?'

'But if he hadn't allowed his tireless work ethic to take him to unproductive places he'd have made more films,' I say. 'For instance the *Space 1999* lawsuit seems, with the benefit of hindsight, a little trivial.'

'Of course I wish he had made more films,' says Jan.

Jan and I are having this conversation inside the stable block, surrounded by hundreds of boxes. For the past few days I have been reading the contents of those marked 'Fan Letters' and 'Résumés'.

They are filled with pleas from hundreds of strangers, written over the decades. They say much the same thing: 'I know I have the talent to be a big star. I know it's going to happen to me one day. I just need a break. Will you give me that break?'

All these letters are – every single one of them – written by people I have never heard of. Many of these young actors and actresses will be middle-aged by now. I want to go back in time and say to them, 'You're not going to make it! It's best you know now rather than face years of having your dreams slowly erode.' They are heartbreaking boxes.

'Stanley never wrote back to the fans,' says Jan. 'He never, never responded. It would have been too much. It would have driven him crazy. He didn't like to get engaged with strangers.'

(In fact, I soon discover, Kubrick did write back to fans, on random, rare occasions. I find two replies in total. Maybe he only ever wrote back twice. One reads, 'Your letter of 4th May was overwhelming. What can I say in reply? Sincerely, Stanley Kubrick.' The other reads, 'Dear Mr William. Thank you for writing. No comment about *A Clockwork Orange*. You will have to decide for yourself. Sincerely, Stanley Kubrick.')

'One time, in 1998,' Jan says, 'I was in the kitchen with Stanley and I mentioned that I'd just been to the opticians in St Albans to get a new pair of glasses. Stanley looked shocked. He said, "Where *exactly* did you go?" I told him and he said, "Oh, thank God! I was just in the other opticians in town getting some glasses and I used your name!"'

Jan laughs.

'He used my name in the opticians, in Waitrose, everywhere.'

'But even if he didn't reply to the fan letters,' I say, 'they've all been so scrupulously read and filed.'

The fan letters are perfectly preserved. They are not in the least bit dusty or crushed. The system used to file them is, in fact, extraordinary. Each fan box contains perhaps fifty orange folders. Each folder has the name of a town or city typed on the front – Agincourt, Ontario; Alhambra, California; Cincinnati, Ohio; Daly City, California, and so on – and are in alphabetical order inside the boxes. And inside each folder are all the fan letters that came from that particular place in any one year. Kubrick has handwritten 'F – P' on the positive ones and 'F – N' on the negative ones. The crazy ones have been marked 'F – C'.

'Look at this,' I say to Jan.

I hand him a letter written by a fan and addressed to Arthur C. Clarke. He forwarded it on to Kubrick and wrote on the top, 'Stanley. See P3!! Arthur.'

Jan turns to page 3, where Arthur C. Clarke marked, with exclamation points, the following paragraph:

What is the meaning behind the epidemic? Does the pink furniture reveal anything about the 3rd mono-lith and it's emitting a pink colour when it first approaches the ship? Does this have anything to do with a shy expression? Does the alcohol offered by the Russians have anything to do with French kiss-ing and saliva?

'Why do you think Arthur C. Clarke marked that particular paragraph for Kubrick to read?' I ask Jan.

'Because it is so bizarre and absurd,' he says.

'I thought so,' I say. 'I just wanted to make sure.'

In the back of my mind I wondered whether this paragraph was marked because the writer of the fan letter – Mr Sam Laks of Alhambra, California – had actually worked out the secret of the monolith in *2001*. I find myself empathizing with Sam Laks. I am also looking for answers to the mysteries. So many conspiracy theories and wild rumours surrounded Kubrick – the one about him being responsible for faking the moon landings (untrue), the one about his terror of germs (this one can't be true either – there's a lot of dust around here), the one about him refusing to fly and drive over 30 mph. (The flying one is true – Tony says he wasn't scared of planes, he was scared of air-traffic controllers, but the one about the 30 mph is 'bullshit', says Tony. 'He had a Porsche.')

This is why my happiest times looking through the boxes are when things turn weird. For instance, at the end of one shelf inside the stable block is a box marked 'Sniper head – scary'. Inside, wrapped in newspaper, is an extremely lifelike and completely disgusting disembodied head of a young Vietnamese girl, the veins in her neck protruding horribly, her eyes staring out, her lips slightly open, her tongue just visible. I feel physically sick looking at it. As I hold it up by its blood-matted hair, Christiane, Kubrick's widow, walks past the window.

'I found a head!' I say.

'It's probably Ryan O'Neal's head,' she replies.

Christiane has no idea who I am, nor what I'm doing in her house, but she accepts the moment with admirable calm.

'No,' I say. 'It's the head of the sniper from *Full Metal Jacket*.'

'But she wasn't beheaded,' calls back Christiane. 'She was shot.'

'I know!' I say.

Christiane shrugs and she walks on.

The sniper head would probably please Mr Sam Laks, on a superficial level, because it is so grotesque. But in general the most exotic things to be found here are generated from the outside, from the imaginations of fans like him.

'I was just talking to Tony about typefaces,' I say to Jan.

'Ah yes,' says Jan. 'Stanley loved typefaces.' Jan pauses. 'I tell you what else he loved.'

'What?' I ask.

'Stationery,' says Jan.

I glance over at the boxes full of letters from people who felt about Kubrick the way Kubrick felt about stationery, and then back to Jan.

'His great hobby was stationery,' he says. 'One time a package arrived with a hundred bottles of brown ink. I said to Stanley, "What are you going to do with all that ink?" He said, "I was told they were going to discontinue the line, so I bought all the remaining bottles in existence." Stanley had a tremendous amount of ink.'

Jan pauses. 'He loved stationery, pads, everything like that.'

Tony Frewin wanders into the stable block.

'How's it going?' he asks.

'Still looking for Rosebud,' I say.

'The closest I ever got to Rosebud,' says Tony, 'was finding a daisy gun that he had when he was a child.'

For months, as I look through the boxes, I don't bother opening the two that read *Shadow on the Sun*. But, one evening just before last Christmas, I decide to take a look.

It is amazing. The boxes contain two volumes of what appears to be a slightly cheesy sci-fi radio drama script. The story begins with a sick dog:

'Can you run me over to Oxford with my dog?' says the dog's owner. 'He's not very well. I'm a bit worried about him, John.'

This is typed.

Kubrick has handwritten below it: 'THE DOG IS NOT WELL.'

It soon becomes clear – through speed-reading – that a virus has been carried to earth on a meteorite. This is why the dog is listless, and also why humans across the planet are no longer able to control their sexual appetites. It ends with a speech:

'There's been so much killing – friend against friend, neighbour against neighbour, but we all know nobody on this earth is to blame, Mrs Brighton. We've all had the compulsions. We'll just have to forgive each other our trespasses. I'll do my part. I'll grant a general amnesty – wipe the slate clean. Then perhaps we can begin to live again, as ordinary decent human beings, and forget the horror of the past few months.'

This too is typed. But all over the script I find notes handwritten by Kubrick. ('Establish Brighton's interest in extra-terrestrial matters.' 'Dog finds meteorite.' 'John has got to have very powerful connections of the highest level.' 'A Bill Murray line!')

'Tony!' I say. 'What the hell is this?'

I believe I have stumbled on a lost Kubrick radio play. Perhaps he did this in his spare time. But if so, why?

'No, no,' says Tony. 'I know what this is.'

Kubrick was always a keen listener to BBC radio, Tony explains. When he first arrived in the UK, back in the early sixties, he happened to hear this drama serial – *Shadow on the Sun*. Three decades later, in the early 1990s, after he had finished *Full Metal Jacket*, he was looking for a new project, so he asked Tony to track the scripts down. He spent a few years, on and off, thinking about *Shadow on the Sun*, reading and annotating the

scripts, before he abandoned the idea and eventually –
after working on and rejecting *AI* – made *Eyes Wide
Shut* instead.

'But the original script seems quite cheesy,' I say.

'Ah,' replies Tony, 'but this is before Stanley worked
his alchemy.'

And I realize this is true. 'Dog finds meteorite'. It
sounds so banal, but imagine how Kubrick might have
directed it. Do the words, 'Ape finds monolith' or 'Little
boy turns the corner and sees twin girls' sound any less
banal on the page?

All this time I have been looking in the boxes for
some embodiment of the fantasies of the outsiders like
Mr Sam Laks and me – but I never do find anything like
that. I suppose that the closer you get to an enigma, the
more explicable it becomes. Even the somewhat crazy-
seeming stuff, like the filing of the fan letters by the town
from which they came, begins to make sense after a
while.

It turns out that Kubrick ordered this filing in case he
ever wanted to have a local cinema checked out. If *2001*,
say, was being screened in Daly City, California, at a
cinema unknown to Kubrick, he would get Tony or one
of his secretaries to telephone a fan from that town to
ask them to visit the cinema to ensure that, say, the
screen wasn't ripped. Tony says that if I'm looking for

something exotic or unexpected or extreme, if I'm looking for the solution to the mystery of Kubrick, I don't
really need to look inside the boxes. I just need to watch
the films.

'It's all there,' he says. 'Those films are Stanley.'

Although the Kubricks always closely guarded their
privacy inside Childwick, I come to the end of my time
at the house during something of a watershed moment.
Christiane Kubrick, and her daughter Katherine, are soon
to open the grounds and the stable block to the public
for an art fair, displaying their work, and the work of a
number of local artists. The boxes are going to be moved
somewhere else. Many, in fact, have now been shipped
to Frankfurt. On 30 March the Deutsche Film Museum
will launch a major Kubrick exhibition, including lenses,
props, cameras and some of the stuff that I found in the
boxes. This will tour across Europe and hopefully visit
London, if the BFI can find a suitable exhibition space.
And the German publishers Taschen are soon to bring
out two books on Kubrick, which will reproduce some
of the Napoleon archive.

Towards the end of my time at the Kubrick house
Tony mentions something that seems inconsequential,
but as soon as he says it I realize that the Rosebud I was
after has been staring me in the face from the very first
day. Right from the beginning I had mentally noted how

well constructed the boxes were, and now Tony tells me that this is because Kubrick designed them himself. He wasn't happy with the boxes that were on the market – their restrictive dimensions and the fact that it was sometimes difficult to get the tops off – so he set about designing a whole new type of box. He instructed a company of box manufacturers, G. Ryder & Co, of Milton Keynes, to construct four hundred of them to his specifications.

'When one batch arrived,' says Tony, 'we opened them up and found a note, written by someone at G. Ryder & Co. The note said, "Fussy customer. Make sure the tops slide off."'

Tony laughs. I half-expect him to say, 'I suppose we *were* a bit fussy.'

But he doesn't. Instead he says, 'As opposed to non-fussy customers who don't care if they struggle all day to get the tops off.'

Unfortunately nobody outside the Kubrick house ever got to see the boxes.